ANOTHER SP

ANOTHER SPRINGTIME

The life of Donald Gee,
Pentecostal leader and teacher

Richard Massey

Highland Books
Guildford, Surrey

Published by Highland Books,
an imprint of Inter Publishing Service (IPS) Ltd,
59 Woodbridge Road, Guildford, Surrey GU1 4RF.

Typeset by Falcon Typographic Art Ltd, Fife, Scotland.
Printed in the UK by HarperCollins Manufacturing, Glasgow.

Contents

To my wife Christine who has encouraged me in writing this book.

Donald Gee – A Tribute

by Michael Harper

I very much hope that this book will encourage a new generation to benefit from the wisdom of the late Donald Gee.

I had the privilege of meeting him several times, and he helped me a great deal to understand and interpret what God was doing in the early stages of the charismatic renewal. The Pentecostals should always feel indebted to this great man's major contribution to their movement. He became a world figure, and helped to build the young movement on firm scriptural foundations, a bulwark against the fanaticism which was to ruin some other branches of the Pentecostal movement.

The first time we met I shared my testimony with him. He was then the Principal of the Assemblies of God College at Kenley. He listened whimsically, and then gave me some sound pieces of advice. The second time was after his retirement to Sussex. This time I was working on a book about the early Pentecostal movement (*As at the Beginning*). He lent me several books, but again it was his wisdom that I remember most. He helped me to gain a balanced understanding of the history of Pentecostalism, but not neglecting the glorious acts of God which have always marked its progress through this century.

I hope very much that Donald Gee will gain new admirers as a result of this book, and that those of us who knew and respected him will be reminded of his major contribution to both the Pentecostal movement and the charismatic renewal.

Preface

An increasing number of people are asking the question : Who was Donald Gee? They may be younger members of the main Pentecostal churches who hear his name mentioned with a kind of respectful awe by older preachers. Or participants in the wide-ranging charismatic renewal movement who read his name in the many books relating to the history and teaching of their movement, usually quoted with appreciation, and wonder who he may have been. Others see some of his books, still widely sold throughout the world, especially in America, and again want to know something about him.

Referring to his role within the twentieth-century Pentecostal movement, Gilbert Kirby, a former principal of London Bible College, stated in a foreword to one of Gee's books:

Undoubtedly Gee was one of the great statesmen of the Movement with which he was so closely associated all his life. His influence and contacts were by no means confined to the British Isles. He was a leading figure at various world conferences of the Pentecostal Movement and knew intimately practically all its leaders. (*Wind and Flame*)

At the time of Gee's death a number of tributes were made capturing some of the breadth of his contribution. John Phillips of the British Assemblies of God described him as follows:

Pioneer, executive, adviser, administrator, Pentecostal ambassador and diplomat; but underlying all these was his fundamental gift of Bible teaching. His anointed ministry plus the power of his pen has been his greatest contribution. (*Redemption Tidings*, 19 August 1966)

In similar vein the Swiss Pentecostal leader, Leonard Steiner, wrote at the same time:

We realise what an outstanding figure he was to the entire Pentecostal movement. What a precious gift of God was his teaching ministry. (*Ibid*)

Although others have written about Donald Gee this book seeks to introduce him to a new generation of readers; both to those within the Pentecostal and charismatic movements and to those from the wider Christian church who wish sympathetically to understand more of those movements. So the book recounts the interesting events of his life, together with his involvement in the progressive stages and development of Pentecostalism.

However, more than anything else, this book aims to be an interpretive biography elucidating and commenting on the teachings and writings of Gee. The author hopes that this constructive drawing together of the main elements of Gee's teaching concerning Pentecostal experience and practice will prove most helpful, and different from other books about Gee. Indeed, a primary aim is to encourage the reading of Gee's books within the new generation of Pentecostal and charismatic groups. For this reason a full bibliography is included at the end of the present work.

For some this book will have a special interest. Those who, like the present author, knew Gee personally will be reminded of his many-sided character and gifted preaching and teaching. For others, especially

members of the British Assemblies of God, it will
provide further insights into the role of the man who
played a leading part in steering that denomination
from its inception in 1924 through to his death in 1966.
His presence in that group brought it international
recognition and status beyond all reference to its actual
size and influence.

I am grateful to the authors of several books which I
have used for background information, not least John
Carter: *Donald Gee – Pentecostal Statesman*; William
Kay: *Inside Story* – a history of the British Assemblies
of God; Colin Whittaker: *Seven Pentecostal Pioneers;*
and Peter Hocken: *Streams of Renewal* – the origins
and early development of the charismatic movement in
Great Britain. Similarly acknowledgement is made to
the Assemblies of God Publishing House, Nottingham,
England and the Gospel Publishing House, Springfield,
Mo., USA for permission to quote from various of Gee's
publications. Finally a tribute to my secretary Valerie
Neame for her patient typing of the material.

As an ongoing recognition of Gee, and to encourage a
wider range of reading and study of Pentecostal issues,
an international research centre has been established
within Mattersey Hall College, Doncaster, England
with the title: *The Donald Gee Centre for Pentecostal
and Charismatic Research*. Most of Gee's materials and
a growing range of other sources are being collected in
the archives at that centre.

I. FORMATIVE YEARS

Chapter 1 – Early Life

Donald Gee was born in May 1891 at Somerfield Road, Finsbury Park in North London and christened Donald Henry Frere Gee. He was the only child of a ticket and show-card writer Henry Gee and followed him in the sign-writing trade. When Donald was nine years old his father died of tuberculosis and so the formative years of his upbringing were spent with his widowed mother Mabel, who carried on the family business in a reasonably prosperous manner combining her considerable artistic and business skills.

As a result Donald had the opportunity of some private schooling, completed by a period at one of the London County Council Board Schools. However, much to his later regret, he never went on to higher education but entered into the family business immediately. Like many of his fellow Pentecostal leaders of that era he was self-taught by reading and study, especially in theology. Later on as a farm labourer during his time as a conscientious objector he sought to master some rudiments of New Testament Greek while working in the fields.

With his mother he attended the thriving Finsbury Park Congregational Church. As a boy of fourteen he was converted in a series of evangelistic meetings conducted by the Welsh preacher Seth Joshua. Gee described the occasion:

On that Sunday night the evangelist asked all who were Christians to rise to their feet. The great majority did so, and I felt very embarrassed.

I knew that I could not honestly stand with
the rest, yet I felt so miserable and conspicuous
sitting down. I remember even trying to achieve
the impossible position of standing up and sitting
down at the same time. Seeing my dilemma, an
elderly lady friend, the wife of one of the deacons,
sitting in the same pew, offered to go out with me
to the enquiry room. She was a timid little soul
herself, but she gave me the needed courage and
we walked out together . . . Re-entering the church
my heart was aglow as I rejoined my mother in
the pew. I knew something had happened in
my heart.

Historians have frequently sought to demonstrate links
between the Welsh Revival of 1904–5 and the beginnings of the Pentecostal movement in Britain. Perhaps
the best that can be said for that theory is that some of
the future Pentecostal leaders such as Donald Gee and
George Jeffreys were converted through the fervent
evangelism created by aspects of that revival. Men
such as Seth Joshua and Evan Roberts paved the
way for Pentecostalism more in terms of recipients
than teaching.

This conversion experience took several years to
mature in Donald's heart and experience. He remained
much more interested in the social and musical side of
his church than in ongoing discipleship. However he
does record that two years after his conversion, particularly through the encouragement of the Christian
Endeavour Society in his church, he consecrated his
life more fully to serving God.

It was his mother who set the spiritual pace for
the family and Donald, who was somewhat shy and
self-conscious, found it all very stressful. Mrs Gee
began to attend a nearby Baptist church and was
eventually baptised by immersion, much to Donald's
embarrassment. Eventually, after some severe inner

struggling, he himself was baptised; his fiancee and wife-to-be, Ruth Clackson, was baptised during the same service. This self-consciousness, despite the bluff outward exterior, was to remain as part of his character; although, after the inner struggles about baptism (of which he said later: 'I felt as if my very reason would snap as a result of the intensity of the spiritual conflict') he never quite faced the same panic again. Nevertheless, perhaps because of the solitary nature of his family situation, or the lack of a higher education, he was to suffer from elements of insecurity and social aloofness. It was later on to show itself even in his own family life, where he found socialising with his young children quite difficult.

However, Donald's mother was not to be limited to an experience of baptism in water. She had met with a missionary, Louise Bowes, working at Pandita Ramabai's Mukti mission in India, who claimed to have been baptised in the Holy Spirit and to have spoken with tongues. This lady had encouraged Mrs Gee to attend some Pentecostal prayer meetings being held in the 'Maranatha' Missionary Rest Home run by Mrs Margaret Cantel in Highbury, London.

Margaret Cantel was in many ways a remarkable woman who exercised considerable influence on the early Pentecostal movement in Britain. She was the daughter of an American named Fielding, who was an elder in Alexander Dowie's church organisation known as Zion City in Illinois. This church group linked in with the emerging Pentecostal movement in the USA and was active in missionary work, especially in South Africa. After marrying one of Dowie's missionary workers, Margaret Cantel came to London with him, but he died in 1912 leaving her with an infant son. Hence she decided to open a Missionary Rest Home to act as a staging post for the many American missionaries *en route* to and from various foreign fields of service. The house she bought, with some members of the Pentecostal Missionary Union Council standing as guarantors, was also large enough to incorporate the small Pentecostal assembly started in Islington by her late husband.

Her home became significant for Donald Gee and his mother in their Pentecostal pilgrimage. Not only were they introduced to the Pentecostal experience, but Donald had the opportunity of meeting and hearing some of the emerging leaders of that movement as they stayed at 'Highbury', as it came to be known colloquially. Later he recalled the house:

> It became for nearly thirty years one of the best known and best beloved of Pentecostal centres not only in London but the whole of the British Isles and far beyond . . . The privacy of the situation lent itself admirably for prolonged meetings for prayer; and those gatherings of a more intimate nature that will always fill a needed place in Christian fellowship and service; while the presence in the home of a constant stream of missionaries and leaders passing through London ensured a rich supply of varied ministry. *(Wind and Flame)*

It was at Highbury in 1913 that he was baptised in the Spirit and indeed where, later on, he preached his first sermon.

Gee had first heard speaking in tongues the previous summer while on holiday in the Isle of Wight with his mother. They had been invited by relatives to attend a small Pentecostal mission in Ryde where the speaker was Ernest Moser of Southsea, a solicitor and member of the Pentecostal Missionary Union Council. Although impressed by the occasion, Donald was also somewhat apprehensive when the invitation to attend the Highbury gatherings was given.

It was mainly to accompany his mother that he attended the first prayer meeting, but the intensity

and reality of the praying caused him to want to be
at future occasions. Shortly afterwards, over a period
of some two weeks, he experienced a baptism in the
Spirit and spoke in tongues.

One Wednesday night in March 1913, I played
for the mid-week service at the Congregational
Church (which finished promptly at 9.00 p.m.),
and ran all the way to enjoy the remainder of
the meeting in Highbury New Park. After it
had concluded (about 10.30 p.m.), the brother
who had been conducting it, a respected minister
from Ireland, put me through a sort of catechism.
'Was I saved?' Yes. 'Was I baptised?' Yes. 'Was
I baptised in the Spirit?' No. 'Then why not?' I
explained my aversion to the apparently weary
'waiting' times. He electrified me by telling me
they were not essential. Opening his Bible he read
to me Luke 11: 13, and then Mark 11: 24, and then
asked me if I believed those verses. I assured him
that I did, and as I declared my faith, it seemed as
if God dropped down in my heart from heaven an
absolute assurance that these promises were now
being actually fulfilled in me. I had no immediate
manifestation, but went home supremely happy,
having received the Baptism of the Holy Spirit
'by faith'. I clearly realised however, that the
experience I had believed God's word for involved
a Scriptural manifestation of the Spirit as in the
Acts, and so I fully expected this, and had no
thought of anything less. From that hour my
joy and gladness were intense, until I hardly
knew how to express myself when in prayer
and praise. The assurance that God had indeed
fulfilled His promise to me gathered in certainty.
I experienced a new fulness beyond words and
found it increasingly difficult to adequately voice
all the glory in my soul. This went on for about

two weeks. Then one night, when praying alone
by my bedside before retiring, and when once
again finding no English adequate to express the
overflowing fulness of my soul, I found myself
beginning to utter words in a new tongue. I was
in a condition of spiritual ecstasy, and taken
up wholly with the Lord. For the first time I
personally tasted the experience referred to in 1
Corinthians 14:2. Increasing glory now flooded my
soul, in the meetings as well, until I began to speak
in new tongues publicly. Also I would sing very
much in the Spirit in new tongues, when the little
assembly would be moved in this way by the Holy
Spirit during our times of prayer and worship. My
whole Christian experience was revolutionised. I
was no longer seeking here and there for spiritual
satisfaction – I had found. (*Redemption Tidings,*
July 1930)

It is interesting to note here Gee's emphasis on the
close links between baptism in the Spirit and speaking
with tongues. He was to become and remain throughout his life a stalwart champion of the so-called 'initial
evidence' teaching that tongues are the paramount
sign of the Pentecostal experience. One can see in his
own testimony that although his experience stretched
over several days, he regarded the occasion of first
speaking with tongues as the conclusion and seal of
that experience.

Speaking at a Pentecostal convention in Kingsway
Hall, London on Whit Monday 1926 he demonstrated
this conviction by observing:

My experience is this, I have never yet known
anybody seeking the fulness of the Holy Spirit
who was finally and completely satisfied until
they had received the evidence of speaking with
tongues.

More will be said of this conviction when we see Gee's part in the formation of the Assemblies of God.

In the same year that he was baptised in the Spirit he was also married to Ruth Clackson, daughter of a local fruiterer and greengrocer. She seems to have provided great encouragement and stability during the difficult years of their wartime experience and early pastoral ministry. Three children, a son and two daughters, were to be born to them; and later Ruth was to exercise her own individual ministry in the Women's Bible College at Louth, Lincolnshire.

Chapter 2 – How Pentecostalism Began

Before we go any further with the story of Gee's early life and beginnings of ministry we need to see the context in which it was happening. A general picture of the emerging Pentecostal movement at the beginning of the twentieth century needs to be seen.

The emergence of the Pentecostal movement in the twentieth-century Christian church has been one of the unusual and fascinating features of modern religious life. This book, though only dealing with one small segment of that movement, nevertheless both contributes to and shares in that interest.

Although Pentecostal Christians assent to the historic doctrines and practices of the Christian church, they also claim to have shared in an experience known as the 'baptism in the Holy Spirit' similar to that of the early Christians on the day of Pentecost. This experience they say is accompanied by various charismata or spiritual gifts, one of which is glossolalia or speaking with tongues.

The movement began in the USA in the first decade of the century and has been characterised by rapid expansion through most countries and affecting almost every Christian denomination. One recent estimate calculates that there may be as many as 60,000,000 members today; the movement has aptly been styled the 'Third Force' in Christianity, alongside Protestantism and Roman Catholicism. This importance was to a large extent created when in the early 1960s the neo-Pentecostal or charismatic movement formed a 'second wind' of Pentecostalism, sweeping through the main Protestant denominations and parts of the Roman Catholic Church. More recently it has led to the House Church movement which, although statistics are difficult to quantify, may well represent a third surge of Pentecostal movement especially influencing the younger generation.

As well as its direct contributions to church life and worship, its restored emphasis on the Holy Spirit in theology and its dynamic input to Christian mission, there is no doubt too that studies of the Pentecostal movement have become a 'growth industry' in terms of books, conferences and research.

By the mid-1920s three groups represented British Pentecostalism: the Elim Pentecostal Alliance, the Apostolic Church and the Assemblies of God. To grasp how they emerged, and to understand the context of Donald Gee's life, it is necessary to examine the rise of Pentecostalism in Britain

Donald Gee in his formative history of Pentecostalism *(Wind and Flame)* observed that in contrast to many other revival movements in Christianity, the Pentecostal movement did not begin with any one outstanding personality or leader 'but was a spontaneous revival appearing almost simultaneously in various parts of the world'. However neither Gee nor any other historian of the movement would claim that there were no background influences leading to the rise of Pentecostalism in the early twentieth century.

Indeed Michael Harper draws attention to the difficulty of tracing the multiplicity of events and sources behind Pentecostalism. It is 'rather like a great river, whose source can be traced back to any one of hundreds of tiny streams in the mountain' *(As at the Beginning)*. Others would see a long line of historical tradition and

experience reaching back to biblical times. So Frederick
Bruner traces Pentecostalism:

> from the enthusiastic Corinthians or even the Old
> Testament anointed ecstatic, through the gnostic
> of all varieties, the Montanists, the medieval
> and pre-Reformation spiritualists, the so-called
> radical, left-wing, or Anabaptist movements, the
> Schwarmer of the Reformation period, the post-
> Reformation Quakers and, when given fresh new
> parentage through the Pietist, Wesleyan and
> revivalist movements of the 17th and 18th Cen-
> turies in Germany, England and the United States,
> continuing in the first half of the 19th Century in
> the higher-life and holiness movements which gave
> birth to their 20th Century child, the Pentecostal
> Movement. *(A Theology of the Holy Spirit)*

The immediate background influence of the nineteenth-
century revivalist and holiness movements seems un-
disputed, especially with their emphasis on a 'two-
stage' or even 'three-stage' process of Christian experience, frequently accompanied by emotional manifestations.

From within the holiness groups emerged Charles
Parham, who began an independent Bible School at
Topeka in Kansas during 1900. A year later several
of his students began to speak with tongues as they
were praying for a baptism with the Holy Spirit. The
importance of this event was the decisive link which
Parham made between baptism in the Spirit and the
sign of glossolalia. Some five years later in 1906 one
of Parham's students, a black pastor named William
Seymour, was at the centre of what most historians
see as the historical beginning of the Pentecostal
movement. It began in Los Angeles when Seymour
taught that baptism in the Spirit should be sought

and that glossolalia should be expected to accompany the experience as a sign. The main centre was a mission hall in Azusa Street where for some three years crowds met regularly to pray and to exercise charismatic phenomena such as glossolalia, prophecy and healing, with black Christians and white Christians worshipping freely together.

Most significantly on this occasion, publicity was given to the happenings in the Christian press. People from different parts of North America and Europe began to visit Azusa Street. Soon whole sections of the American Holiness churches were won over to this new experience and were teaching a 'three-stage' pattern of Christian life: conversion, sanctification and baptism in the Spirit. Non-Holiness groups such as the Assemblies of God came into being, teaching two stages only: conversion and baptism in the Spirit. It had become evident that a major renewal movement and a new direction in American religious life was taking place.

Of course this movement was not limited to the USA, and soon it was to reach the British Isles.

The nineteenth-century background to the British Pentecostal movement was very similar to that of the USA, with revivalist and 'higher-life' emphases quite prominent through the ministry of evangelist Dwight L. Moody and the Keswick Convention. However, the most effective background and contributory factor appears to have been the so-called Welsh Revival of 1904–5. Although in the revival there was no direct evidence of glossolalia, it nevertheless provided a spirit of expectation in the rest of Britain and many of the Pentecostal leaders of the future movement were influenced by it, including Alexander Boddy. It was, as Frederick Bruner aptly observes, 'the last "gap" across which the latest sparks of holiness enthusiasm leapt, igniting the Pentecostal movement'.

One of the main figures in the beginning of the British Pentecostal movement was a Norwegian Methodist minister, Thomas B. Barrett. Actually Barrett had links with Britain beforehand, in that he was born in Cornwall in 1862 and then moved with his father, a mining engineer, to Norway. During the early years of Barrett's ministry he had searched for a deeper experience of the Holy Spirit, in the process writing to Evan Roberts, the leader of the Welsh Revival, enquiring about 'a further baptism of fire'.

He had gone to America to raise funds for his Oslo City Mission church in 1906 and was attracted by reports of the Los Angeles Azusa Street revival. Although not visiting Los Angeles itself, Barrett began to seek the Pentecostal experience and appears to have received the baptism in the Spirit in two stages. First of all on 7 October he privately prayed and fasted until he was 'seized by the Holy Power of God', and then on 16 November he experienced glossolalia after other Christians had laid hands upon him. After Barrett returned to Norway he began to preach and write of his experience and a strong Pentecostal movement emerged in Scandinavia under his influence.

The decisive link with Britain came through Alexander Boddy. This former solicitor was the Anglican vicar of All Saints Church, Monkswearmouth in Sunderland. He was a regular visitor to the Keswick Conventions and had made several visits to Wales to examine the revival happenings there at first hand. On reading Barrett's account of Pentecostal events in Norway, he had travelled to Oslo and been greatly impressed. Boddy pressed Barrett to come to Sunderland, which he did in August 1907, staying for some six weeks. This period was a watershed in British religious life. Continuous meetings were held in Sunderland. Several people, including Boddy and his family, received a baptism in the Spirit accompanied by glossolalia. As the press began to report these happenings, so Christians from all over Britain journeyed to Sunderland to investigate and share in them.

Barrett's momentous visit established Sunderland as the main pre-war centre of British Pentecostalism and inaugurated Boddy as its unrivalled leader. As Harper notes, Sunderland did for Britain what Azusa Street had done for America. Moreover the annual Whitsuntide conventions at Sunderland and the regular publication of the magazine *Confidence*, edited by Boddy, continued to stimulate and direct the growth of Pentecostalism in Britain for some two decades.

Other figures, though initially of lesser stature than Boddy, played a part in this development. Cecil Polhill, a wealthy landowner from Bedfordshire and former member of the China Inland Mission and the Cambridge Seven group, had gone personally to Los Angeles Azusa Street Mission in 1907. While there he too had received a baptism in the Spirit and spoken in tongues. When he returned to Britain he soon became associated with Boddy. Polhill's main contributions to the early Pentecostal movement in Britain were to give it a missionary dimension – notably through the commencement of the Pentecostal Missionary Union in 1909 – considerable financial support, and a 'London dimension' especially through the weekly Sion College Friday-night Pentecostal meetings which he organised; if Sunderland had a weakness, it was in its awkward geographical location.

Another British leader was Smith Wigglesworth who brought a bluff but dynamic evangelistic emphasis to the movement, not least with his remarkable ministry of faith-healing. Similarly within a few years men of the organisational and mission calibre of George Jeffreys and William Burton had also appeared on the scene of British Pentecostalism. Nevertheless, as Donald Gee observed, it was Boddy who:

... was God's man for the onerous task of presid-
ing over the early British Pentecostal Conventions
and for a few years was the outstanding personality of the movement. He had the prestige, the
poise, the culture and the personal participation
in the Pentecostal experience that established him
as the figure-head. *(Wind and Flame)*

This situation of a rather loose affiliation of individuals
and Pentecostal groups – held together by attendance
at Conventions, support for the Pentecostal Missionary
Union and the itinerant ministries of various evangelists and teachers – lasted until the outbreak of
World War I. However, by the end of the first decade
of Pentecostalism the groups were larger and more
numerous; various gifted leaders were appearing on
the scene and in general Pentecostal believers were
receiving little encouragement in their own denominations. Against this background various Pentecostal
denominations began to emerge; notably the Elim
Pentecostal Alliance, the Apostolic Church and the
Assemblies of God.

The story of the Elim Pentecostal Alliance is very
much the story of George Jeffreys and to a lesser
extent his brother Stephen. George Jeffreys was a
product of the Welsh Revival. He was brought up in
the Maestag 'Shiloh' Congregational Chapel where
his minister soon recognised his ability. In 1910 he
met up with the Pentecostal groups and received
a baptism in the Spirit in that year. During 1912,
through the financial aid of Cecil Polhill, he was
able to study at the Pentecostal Missionary Union
Men's Training College in Preston under Thomas
Myerscough. He emerged from Preston and began to
conduct a series of evangelistic campaigns in which he
displayed great abilities as a revivalist preacher and
biblical expositor. Gee notes that he had 'a voice of great
musical ability as a preacher, striking appearance, and

that subtle quality known as "personality"' *(Wind and Flame)*.

A turning point came for him in 1914 when he conducted a series of successful meetings in Ireland. It was there in 1915 in the town of Monaghan that together with other members of his team he decided to form the Elim Evangelistic Band, with the purpose of permanent evangelistic work in Ireland. Later in the same year the first Elim Hall in Britain was purchased in Belfast. By 1920 some twenty buildings had been obtained in Ireland. For legal purposes the denomination was more formally established in 1918 under the name of the Elim Pentecostal Alliance.

Although the Elim group shared much in common with the other Pentecostal groups, its distinguishing feature was a tightly-knit, centralised form of church government, revolving around the somewhat autocratic figure of Jeffreys. In the early 1920s he began to expand the Elim work into England, and the next two decades were a growth period in Britain for the Elim churches. However, it was confrontation with this somewhat rigid centralised pattern of church life that caused some Pentecostal leaders to feel that a safeguard against such a system was needed for the independent assemblies, which was one reason for the formation of the Assemblies of God.

The Apostolic Church is the smallest of the three main British Pentecostal denominations. It began as the Apostolic Faith Church in Bournemouth under the leadership of William Hutchinson. Differences of opinion about church government led to many leaving and forming a new centre at Penygroes in South Wales in 1916 under the leadership of Daniel P. Williams. Eventually in 1922 three other churches holding similar views in Glasgow, Bradford and Hereford joined with the Penygroes group to form the Apostolic Church. Their distinctive emphasis was on the recognition and appointment of apostles and prophets who guided the

church and individuals by their revelations. In the early
1920s the Apostolic Church was active in proselytising
among other Pentecostal groups, especially in Wales.
This caused considerable alarm and again became a
factor in the formation of the Assemblies of God. In
the light of the part Donald Gee was to play in it, it is
a story that needs a fuller treatment. However, before
that, more of the early life of Donald Gee himself needs
to be sketched.

Chapter 3 – Conscientious Objection

At the time of Donald Gee's early involvement with the
Pentecostal movement through the Highbury Missionary Rest Home, the same meetings were being attended
by Albert Saxby, the minister of a Baptist church in
Harringay, North London. After he had been baptised
in the Spirit, Saxby met hostility and opposition in his
own church. This grew with what Gee described later as
'unbelievable scenes of deliberate disorder' eventually
leading to some form of mediation by the Secretary of
the Baptist Union.

When the church organist resigned in protest Donald
offered to take his place. This was to be the beginning of
several formative and eventful years in his life as he sat
regularly under Saxby's ministry. There is little doubt
that Saxby was a fine biblical preacher and became
Gee's role model for his own later teaching ministry.
Although they were to part company in the early 1920s
because of Saxby's false views – he embraced a form
of universalism known as the doctrine of ultimate
reconciliation – nevertheless Gee appears to have taken
much from him in terms of general biblical doctrine and
Pentecostal teaching.

In 1915 Saxby found staying in his Baptist church
intolerable and so the congregation sadly divided.
After a short time in rented halls a new church was
built in Harringay, known as Derby Hall. Donald Gee
and his wife became members of this independent
Pentecostal assembly. It was in this assembly and in

similar London ones that Donald began to develop his preaching ministry and skills. As Saxby's talents led him more into major Pentecostal convention ministry, particularly at Kingsway Hall where Cecil Polhill had commenced such gatherings, Donald was invited to be the organist and so was in the forefront of those vivid meetings.

Perhaps the most challenging of all emphases in Saxby's assembly was that upon pacifism during the period of World War I. Gee identified the origin of this stance as the close connections of Saxby with the Quaker pacifist, Arthur Booth-Clibborn, son-in-law of General Booth the founder of the Salvation Army.

There was no official Pentecostal line on conscientious objection to war among the various assemblies, but as Gee noted, 'it precipitated a personal issue of deep gravity for many young men among Pentecostal believers'. An interesting illustration of those varying attitudes is given by Frank Bartleman, an American Pentecostal leader who visited London in 1914. He writes:

I spoke once at the Central Pentecostal Mission. The Lord gave me a strong message against the War spirit in Christians. The leader (possibly Cecil Polhill) said if he were a young man he would enlist himself. They were opening their meetings with a 'War Hymn' . . . my message dropped like a bomb (sic) in the camp.

Then by contrast, shortly afterwards, he spoke in Saxby's church:

Here God gave me a strong message against the War spirit also. But it was very differently received. The leader thanked me warmly.'

So in 1916, when conscription was introduced, Donald

Gee decided that he would be a conscientious objector.
He duly appeared before an examining tribunal in
Stoke Newington. After a series of questions, including
one from a clergyman asking whether he would be
equally willing to be a foreign missionary – a decision
he had already made some years previously, despite
his timidity towards such a role – the tribunal accepted
his objection and ordered him to find work of national
importance.

Gee never wrote a complete autobiography but
towards the end of his life he began to write a form of
memoir entitled *Pentecostal Pilgrimage*, which provides
an interesting vignette of his time as a conscientious
objector. It is well worth recording in some detail as an
important foundational time in Gee's life.

My experiences as a conscientious objector never
took me farther than Oxford, but they cut so
deeply into my heart and life that the effect was
indelible. If ever I had any direct training for
the work of the ministry it was certainly during
those three unforgettable years when I became
a farm-labourer. I was placed by Providence in
God's own 'school', and have felt thankful for it
ever since. The Tribunal in London granted me
exemption from military service on condition that
I took up some work of National Importance to
their satisfaction within fourteen days. The snag
was that I had to find such work for myself. The
alternative was imprisonment.

Now my wife had an uncle with a small dairy-
farm near High Wycombe, Bucks. We had enjoyed
one or two holidays there. At once I wrote to this
relative to enquire if he knew of any local farmer
who would be willing to give me employment. To
our complete surprise we received a telegram in
reply – 'Come down at once and arrange'. When
I got to Lane End I found that our uncle was

urgently needing a man himself, and that he had no objection to employing a hated 'conchie'. So I notified my Tribunal of my employment and employer, and had no obligation to add that it was a relative. Exactly two weeks afterwards I started on my new job, and felt truly that the Lord had undertaken for us in a wonderful way.

A small cottage in what was known as 'Rasherfat Row' went with my new job as part of its remuneration. My uncle had no intention of treating me any differently from the other labourers, and indeed neither did I wish him to do so, nor would it have been wise. My wife, with our two months' old first baby, soon followed me with as much of our furniture as the cottage would contain. I can never speak too appreciatively of the way she has stuck to me all through our chequered career, with never a grumble or moan. Fortunately our hearts have been one because we were married 'in the Lord', and from the very first shared the baptism in the Holy Spirit and willing consecration to do the will of God. My wages at Lane End were exactly £1 per week. We had always tithed our income, and now continued to do, though faced with the problem of making 'both ends meet' on 18 shillings a week. 'Jehovah-Jireh' did not fail us.

Among the noteworthy ways in which we felt that God supplied our needs at that time of happy poverty was through the potato patch. The U boat attack was at its height, and to make matters worse there was a complete potato famine, for rationing had been delayed for too long in that first world war. But along with our cottage I was given a rather poor piece of garden that had previously been cropped with potatoes. These had been lifted very carelessly, and consequently, as I proceeded to dig it over, I brought up quite useful potatoes with every turn of the fork. In that way we never lacked potatoes for many weeks, even while our neighbours had great difficulty though they were experienced gardeners. Our milk came to us cheaply, as part of my wages, and that helped us where the baby was concerned. I had quickly learned to milk the cows night and morning. Utter physical exhaustion brought real suffering during the first year of my work on the land. My business in London had been sedentary, and the change of work was drastic. Many a time when ploughing with the horses I could thankfully have flung myself down on the hard ground for a few moments rest. In the harvest days we worked as much as sixteen or seventeen hours, and there were some nights when I crawled home to the cottage only to burst into tears on my wife's shoulder through nothing but sheer fatigue. It was a discovery that physical tiredness could mean absolute pain. In those hard, though healthy, years I slept like the proverbial log. Gradually I settled down into the slow dogged rhythm of all work on the land, and became toughened to it enough to do my share with the rest.

It was the social suffering as a hated 'conchie' that went deeper however. Except for some fellow-Christians I soon found that I was a complete social outcast. Boys delighted to throw stones and dirt at me along the road: men and women vented their spite in venomous words and open threats. Sometimes at night they would stand outside our cottage and shout their taunts after we had retired for the night. I welcomed work on the more secluded parts of the farm, especially if I could be all alone. As an only child from birth I had grown up with a deep inward sensitiveness and shyness that few realised. Unfriendly treatment that others would have taken little notice of was mental torture to me. Often I was inclined to envy

my friends who had been sent to prison. To my
imagination they were passing through a more
sheltered ordeal than my own in a village. And
I suppose that they, in their turn, were tempted
to envy me.

Only God knows what I suffered in my soul
at that time. Yet I now know that He used
it to put some needed iron into my character.
Both physically and spiritually I gained at least
some measure of manliness under that stern
curriculum. Neither could I blame my persecutors.
They were mostly the kind of folk who could have
no kind of appreciation of the grounds on which
I based my conscientious objection to military
service. Their own sons, and husbands, and fathers
were all away in the filth and constant danger of
the trenches at the various fronts. The casualty
lists after the battles on the Western Front were
appalling. Moreover in the war of 1914–1918 the
civilian population in England dwelt in compara-
tive safety. There were only a few Zeppelin raids.
All that my neighbours in Buckinghamshire saw
in me was a young man, perfectly fit, who was
escaping the perils and sufferings of their own
loved ones. No wonder they hated the sight of me. I
could not but appreciate their point of view, though
it made my mental suffering all the harder.

My chief solace was fellowship with the Christians in local chapels and mission-halls. At first
I missed more deeply than can be put into words
the Pentecostal fellowship of the little assembly
in London of which I had been a member from
its inception. More than I realised I had lived my
spiritual life on, and in, its meetings. Now I was
to learn to walk alone with God, but the discipline
was very unwelcome.

The local Methodists soon discovered that I had
been an organist, and they gave me a cordial

welcome, which I also cordially accepted, to become
their organist and choirmaster for that first winter
of our 'exile'. We had some good times, and the
choir-practices became quite a little 'Pentecostal'.
When passing through High Wycombe I had often
noticed a Holiness Mission, and when opportunity
offered I attempted to find there what I thought
would prove to be a more congenial spiritual
fellowship. It was a cycle ride of only four miles.
But among the good Holiness people I soon found
myself marked as a dangerous member of the
dreaded 'Tongue Movement'. My reception was
decidedly mixed. Only on one occasion was I
allowed on to their platform, and then one of
the leading sisters sat in the front row with
her eyes shut, her face set like steel under her
little blue bonnet, and her lips moving in silent
prayer against me all the time I was trying to
speak. Such is prejudice. It can hardly be said
that I enjoyed much liberty of utterance there.
That Mission, though it owned a beautiful hall,
shut down completely a very few years later.

Nevertheless, as God would have it, my contacts with that Holiness Mission provided a most
important link in the chain of events. After less
than a year at Lane End my wife's uncle died,
the farm was sold, and I had quickly to secure
employment elsewhere to maintain the terms of
my exemption. Among the farmers who attended
the Holiness meetings a noticeable figure was
Henry Simmons, who farmed the two hundred
and thirty acres of famous old 'Pophleys' right on
the summit of the Chiltern Hills at Stokenchurch.
He was a remarkable character in several ways – a
keen Christian, a man of considerable culture and
independence of thought, and a gentleman-farmer
of the old school. Already I had discovered him to
be free from the prejudices of most of the other

members of the Holiness Mission. To 'Pophleys'
therefore, one lovely summer's evening, I cycled
seeking renewed employment and found them
combating a fire in a new hay-rick! In spite of
that embarrassment, Mr Simmons received me
courteously and forthwith engaged me as one of
his hands. A farm-wagon was sent over for our
goods, and very soon my wife and I, with the
baby, found ourselves installed in a newly-built
cottage in the corner of a meadow, seven hundred
feet above sea-level. There, the next year, our son
was born.

Work now became harder than ever. My uncle's
farm had been a little amateur affair compared
with this large arable farm that, owing to the
war, was cruelly under-staffed. It was little short
of slavery for all of us, the master included, except
during the short winter days. All year round we
commenced in the stables at 5 a.m. After a break
for breakfast we were expected to be out in the
fields to start ploughing at 7 a.m. On dark winter
mornings I have stood under a hedge waiting for
it to become light enough to work. To such folly
can tradition bind employers. We had a short
interval for lunch for ourselves and the horses
at 11 a.m., and went home for a more substantial
meal at 3 p.m. Then back for all the routine work
with the cattle and livestock, finishing soon after
5 p.m. in the winter, and working progressively
longer hours as the daylight grew. There were no
half-days, and no public holidays, and the only
difference on Sundays was that we had only the
livestock to attend to. But that took some hours,
and left only time for a short interlude in the
middle of the day. For all that we were paid,
when I left the land, and after it became legally
binding, the sum of 33 shillings a week, plus a
cottage and a few extras off the farm. Yet the

older hands with whom I worked had brought up their families on as little as 13 shillings a week. It would have been impossible had not the purchasing power of money been greater in those days. Even so, it was a mere pittance, and none can wonder that it turned a younger generation against the most vital industry of our nation.

God had other business for me at 'Pophleys' than merely manual labour, exacting though that was. I soon found that Mr Simmons liked to arrange the work, if possible, so that he and I could have some quiet conversation together while working. He questioned me closely about our Pentecostal testimony. One day, while we were working strenuously together on top of a hay-rick, receiving and placing the stuff as it came up at the elevator in a ceaseless stream, I preached the baptism in the Holy Spirit to him for all I was worth. The happy sequel occurred some weeks later when Mr and Mrs Simmons came round to our cottage one evening for a time of waiting upon God. The power of God fell on my employer, but we were surprised to see him taking off his jacket as though in the field. He seemed oblivious to his surroundings. Soon we heard him speaking with tongues as the Spirit gave him utterance, and our little cottage-room became the very gate of heaven. When, at a late hour, our guests were leaving for their own home, my employer volunteered the information that, to him, the 'Fire' in the baptism of the Holy Ghost and fire, had seemed so literally fulfilled that he instinctively took off his jacket for physical relief. In fact the sweat had stood upon his forehead.

But this gracious working of God with my employer was far from all. Near the farm, in the sweet little scattered village of Radnage, was a Free Mission Hall built and conducted by a

company of earnest, simple evangelical Christians
who had felt compelled to leave the neighbouring
Chapels as a protest against their worldliness and
declension. Among these friends we felt instantly
at home, and received a hearty welcome. Our
message concerning the Second Coming of the
Lord Jesus was quite new truth to them, and they
received it enthusiastically. Then we unfolded to
them the full testimony of Pentecost. Tarrying
meetings now commenced in our cottage during
the winter months in earnest, and the Lord met
and filled with His Spirit quite a few hungry souls.
Quite undesignedly my wife and I were entering
into Pentecostal ministry. Incidentally we also
were proving how faithfully the Lord supplies
every need. After those cottage prayer-meetings
we would find purposely left for us under the
chairs various little helpful gifts; here two or three
eggs; there a small packet of butter; under another
chair something from market. When a paraffin oil
famine was at its height we even found, one night,
a small bottle of paraffin.

On Sunday evenings I often was called to preach
the word. Owing to the amount of work on the
farm with the livestock it sometimes meant me
proceeding straight to the Hall in my corduroy
breeches and leather leggings – but we all cared
little about that! It brought an unexpected spice
of excitement one Sunday night, however, when
the local policeman first of all stood outside the
Mission Hall and then, when I began to preach,
came in and sat very officially in the back row to
discover whether the hated conscientious-objector
was promulgating treason. He heard nothing but
the gospel, and I think personally disliked his
task, but he had been sent by local 'gentry'
who wanted to do anything to get me removed.
In after years, when I had exactly the same

experience while preaching in our Polish Assemblies of God, my Eastern European friends were surprised indeed when I cut short their apologies by telling them that I had already suffered a similar ordeal in England. My ministerial training in Buckinghamshire was more complete than I ever guessed at the time.

There came at last a grey, misty November morning in 1918 when I was working all alone in the fields at 'Pophleys'. At 11 a.m. I heard the distant sirens at the chair-factories, and knew that the Armistice had been signed, and the war was over and I realised at last I was free. But almost we were ready to stay on now indefinitely. Our hearts had become entwined with the little company of believers we had been allowed to lead into fuller life and light in Bucks. My patient boss was thankful, however, for the prospect of at last securing more competent help on the farm. I never shone as an agricultural labourer. To this day tales are told of my misadventures – how old Punch backed both the horse-rake and myself into a prickly hedge, how I dropped the bucket into the water-tank, and various other amusing evidences that, at best, I was a clumsy townsman. We had to prepare to leave 'Pophleys'. But to where? Steadily, and with increasing strength, the conviction had grown in our hearts during those years on the land, that God was calling us to devote our time wholly to the work of the ministry.

Chapter 4 – Beginnings of Ministry

By the end of the war Donald Gee was already twenty-seven years old and the father of two small children, Winifred and David. However, there were to be more years of patient waiting before his first opportunity for pastoral ministry. Thus for a while he found himself back in London desperately trying to make ends meet through his old trade of ticket-writing; and they were occasionally forced to sell some wedding presents given before the war.

His preaching ministry continued in various Pentecostal assemblies. He often cycled up to ten miles for a Sunday appointment and was grateful for the small fee given for his expenses. Yet these years were looked back on by Gee as being of great value for his full-time service. He spoke of being firmly convinced that the best training a minister could have was within the framework of a normal local assembly under the direction of a competent pastor. Similarly his business experience taught him self-discipline, personal organisation and – as he expressed it – how to 'live by faith'.

Sometimes his preaching invitations took him out of London. On one such weekend at Eastbourne he received an unexpected telegram from his pastor, Albert Saxby, asking if he would consider going to a small Pentecostal Assembly in Edinburgh where they were looking for a minister. Saxby was taking some services in that assembly and the elders had asked if he himself would stay or could recommend someone else to be their pastor.

Thus in June 1920 Gee set off alone on the 'Flying Scotsman' to travel to Edinburgh, and then on to the port of Leith on the banks of the river Forth. Here he was met by Eilif Beruldsen, the founder of the Leith Pentecostal assembly, in whose home Donald would stay until accommodation could be arranged for his wife and children to join him.

Beruldsen was a Norwegian sea-captain who had married the daughter of a Scottish harbour-master. He eventually gave up the sea and became a prosperous ship-chandler in the port of Leith. Originally he was an elder of Charlotte Chapel, a large Baptist church in Edinburgh. However after visiting Sunderland in 1907 to hear the Pentecostal leader Thomas Barrett from Oslo preaching in the Anglican church of Alexander Boddy, he was baptised in the Spirit. This led to difficulties with his church and he decided to begin a small Pentecostal assembly in Leith. During the ten years or so that followed the assembly was zealous but never really grew, because of lack of pastoral leadership and suffering from some of the divisions affecting many early Pentecostal groups. Nevertheless it did develop a strong missionary concern and three of Beruldsen's children went to China with the Pentecostal Missionary Union.

Gee's heart sank a little when he first saw the unattractive, low-roofed, double-fronted shop in Bridge Street, which had been rented by Beruldsen as an assembly meeting place and mission hall. However he was elated at his first pastoral opportunity and convinced of God's calling not to be downcast. His first sermon on the Sunday morning following his arrival on the Saturday also encouraged him. Only about a dozen people were there and he preached on Isaiah 40:1, 'Comfort ye, comfort ye my people.' This was just the message the troubled and divided assembly needed; Gee's pastoral instinct enabled him to get off on the right foot with the church that was to be his responsibility for the next twelve years.

The story of those twelve years is delightfully documented in Gee's small book *Bonnington Toll*. Its value lies not only in the interesting description of Gee's ministry in Edinburgh but it is also a remarkable account and insight into the life of one of the early British Pentecostal assemblies, 'warts and all'. Few such descriptions exist; moreover it is perhaps one of the best examples of Gee's fine prose style.

Gee was to stay for five weeks with the Beruldsen family on a kind of probation, though it was up to Donald and the Beruldsens rather than the assembly whether he should stay or not. The decision was taken that he should remain. He went to London to bring Ruth and the children back to Scotland.

Housing was a difficulty at this time. Renting involved waiting lists; purchase was financially impossible. After a while they managed to rent a small top floor flat which had, typically for Scotland at that time, a bed in the kitchen. When in eighteen months' time they were desperate for larger accommodation, a member of their assembly bought a small house on their behalf and rented it to them. The rest of the Gee's furniture was moved up from London to 3 Scotland Street, Leith, where the family was to remain for some ten years.

It could not be said that Donald Gee's time at Leith was a brilliant success story, although it was by no means a failure. Rather, as often happens in a first pastorate, it was to be a time of learning, of laying personal foundations in ministry and the springboard of opportunity for the future. Gee adopted an established routine of morning study and writing from which he was to vary only occasionally throughout his busy life. Those entertaining him in their homes later on often thought him either shy or rude, because he would bring his typewriter with him and work away in his bedroom rather than socialise with his hosts.

He describes how he quickly set up a small study in his church and morning by morning cycled there for three hours of study and devotion. Later on when reminiscing about these earlier years he expressed a wish that he had read more widely than he did and learned one or two foreign languages. Gee's study room in later years at Kenley Bible College, where he was principal, never had a great display of books. He used the commentaries of Matthew Henry and Campbell Morgan and he frequently quoted Alexander Whyte's writings. It is interesting to speculate whether his fondness for Whyte, the famous minister of Free St George's in Edinburgh, stemmed from the fact that Gee learned that Whyte had also lived in Scotland Street as a student.

One of the most valuable disciplines that Gee mastered in those study times was that of writing. There was obviously a flair for writing in his personality, but in order to develop it he would write an essay each morning for half-an-hour on any subject that caught his attention. Most of the essays were thrown into his waste-paper basket but the marshalling of ideas and the lucidity of expression were to form the foundations of an important ministry of books and journalism. It is probable that one of those essays became the first published article by Donald Gee, to be found in the *Elim Evangel* magazine in January 1922 and entitled 'Belief and Faith'. Many hundreds of similar articles were to find their way into Pentecostal magazines all over the world alongside several books and pamphlets, culminating in 1947 with his editorship of the first international Pentecostal journal: *Pentecost*.

Although Edinburgh in the 1920s was somewhat remote from other main centres of Pentecostalism, Gee determinedly both kept and developed links with key leaders of the movement. As a result of a legacy to his

wife from an aunt, they were able to buy a motorcycle
and side-car and later on a small car. This enabled Gee
to travel, not frequently but at least regularly, to some
of the London and Preston conventions as well as to
the Pentecostal leaders' conferences organised by his
former pastor, Saxby, at Swanwick in Derbyshire. More
importantly for Gee's contacts were the invitations he
gave to preach in his own church to a wide range of
Pentecostal leaders such as George Jeffreys, William
Burton and Smith Wigglesworth.

On the other hand, Gee does not seem to have
cultivated close relationships with Alexander Boddy
in Sunderland, who was the foremost British leader.
This was more by force of circumstances than because of
any major personal differences. Boddy was growing old
and a newer generation of leaders was emerging. Moreover, since the First World War both the Sunderland
Conventions and *Confidence*, the magazine edited
by Boddy, were in decline. Although Gee's pacifism
would not have enamoured him to Boddy, it was to be
Boddy's reluctance to form some kind of Pentecostal
denomination or organisation that created the greatest
rift between him and the younger generation of leaders.
If anything, the original British leaders such as Boddy
and Polhill were bypassed rather than overthrown.

One of the most significant opportunities for Gee
came in January 1921 when he was asked by Einar
Beruldsen, the eldest son of the Beruldsen family,
to accompany him to the International Pentecostal
Convention in Amsterdam. Although one or two earlier
international conventions had been held in Sunderland
and Germany, this was the first since the war. Its tensions lay in the sort of response the leaders would make
to each other, especially the German delegates, and the
challenges of the new post-war era for Pentecostalism
as a developing movement. But for Gee one of its main
attractions was that it was his first trip abroad. He particularly noted Holland's colourful houses in contrast

with Edinburgh's greyness, the intensive cultivation of the land and the first taste of real coffee.

The conference was hosted by pastor George Polman, the Dutch leader, at the Immanuel Pentecostal Church in Kerkstraat, Amsterdam. Gee seems to have been impressed with the way that some of the Pentecostal groups on the continent had already obtained large attractive buildings; by comparison, Scotland was still in 'the day of small things'.

It was not a particularly memorable conference for its content, and it almost became bogged down in the Germans' insistence on an experience of personal sanctification through 'dying to self' as being a complementary part of the Pentecostal experience. For the first time we begin to see some of Gee's practical and balanced understanding of theology emerging, which was to be a hallmark of his later leadership. He assessed the various 'mystical interpretations' of Scripture given by the German group as 'boring and unconvincing'. With shrewd insight he went on:

> It was all far too negative and lacked the compensating positive of new 'life' in Christ. Unconsciously to themselves they were suffering from depression consequent upon their defeat in the war, and wanted to impose their own emotional condition upon us all, under the guise of spiritual experience.

What indeed was memorable for him and formed an important connection for his future travels was the meeting with various international leaders. Gee quickly established personal links with Lewi Pethrus of Sweden and the German leaders Paul and Voget, but especially with the Swiss leader, Henry Steiner, of whom he commented 'We were mutually attracted immediately and that first meeting blossomed into a lifelong friendship.' Gee's overall assessment of the

visit when he returned to Scotland was that his 'mental
and spiritual horizons had been broadened', and that
although seven more years were to pass before he
would travel abroad again, his 'vision and contacts
were becoming worldwide'.

Of course Gee had his difficulties at Leith and they
too were part of his maturing process. Finance was
always a problem in the early years. Perhaps drawing
on his previous business experience, Gee introduced
into his assembly the practice of being personally
responsible for the church's finance. He left a box at the
rear of the hall and met the bills for the church from it.
Whatever remained over was for his own upkeep. Each
week he would write the amount in the box on a small
blackboard, leaving the members to draw their own
conclusions. Looking back today this does not seem particularly wise of Gee, but in those early times of stress it
seems to have given him the security of independence.

The problem was not helped when in 1921 a rent rise
on the church mission hall caused them to take the
step of faith to build their own church. Eilif Beruldsen
gave them a small piece of land in nearby Bonnington
Toll and by January 1922 a new wooden hall had been
erected. It was to be known simply as Bonnington Toll
Hall. However in 1923 the Beruldsen family decided to
emigrate to Australia, thus removing Gee's underlying
financial support and the moral support in his pastoral
work of a godly, if paternalistic, family.

At the beginning of 1923 accumulated pastoral tensions, brought about in Gee's assembly by ill-disciplined
behaviour and aggressive proselytism from various
Pentecostal factions in Scotland such as the Apostolic
churches, caused him to flee to London for two weeks.
Whether this was some sort of nervous breakdown
or not, it was certainly a crisis. If anything Gee was
over-conscientious in those years; he had set himself a
gruelling schedule of meetings held almost every night
in his assembly as well as monthly conventions. This,

coupled with his study and writing, all came to a head
as financial and pastoral problems reached excessive
levels. The problem was solved on one hand by complete
rest in London for two weeks and talking matters
through with old friends – possibly Albert Saxby
and Margaret Cantel. On the other hand he was
considerably helped in his own assembly just before he
fled to London by the preaching of Howard Carter, one
of the most able teachers among the rising generation
of British Pentecostal leaders. Carter had touched on
the subject at the heart of Gee's crisis, namely the role
and need of the teaching gift in Pentecostalism. Gee,
who was a balanced and gifted biblical teacher, was
constantly criticised for emphasising this ministry by
those who only wanted more or less unchecked worship
and superficial experience. In his later writings Gee
was to give prominence to teaching as a charismatic gift
in its own right. Similarly he was to be highly critical of
those who saw the sum total of Pentecostalism only in
terms of healing evangelism.

The culmination of these difficulties and tensions
came in an unusual happening in the life of one who
was to be an outstanding leader of the Assemblies
of God – an application to join the Elim Pentecostal
Alliance in 1923. It appears that Gee was anxious to
gain security both for himself and his assembly by
exploring the possibility of joining George Jeffreys'
Elim organisation which had been established mainly
in Ireland since 1915, but had begun to add churches
in mainland Britain since the end of the war.

In his own writings Gee barely mentions this dialogue with Elim, but it is well documented in a series
of letters between him and the Elim leaders. To
Gee's credit, his firm stand on his personal principles
comes through at the end of what could have been
an embarrassment. This correspondence is well worth
noting because of the interesting insights it gives into
Gee's personality and circumstances at this time.

Gee had always maintained close links with the Elim movement and its leaders. In fact, he had visited various Elim churches in Ireland shortly before his first letter of approach to them, and it may well have been this visit that finally convinced him of the value of belonging to such an organisation. On 23 March 1923 he wrote from Edinburgh to William Henderson of the Elim Pentecostal Alliance Council in Belfast as follows:

> I am writing to you with regard to the work here becoming properly associated with the Elim Pentecostal Alliance. I do not know yet, of course, whether you are willing for this on your side, but if so I should be glad if you would very kindly let me know just what such a step would entail both for the Assembly and for myself personally as the pastor.

Gee went on to give his reasons for this move:

> I believe myself, that some such step is necessary before we can see the measure of prosperity here that we long for, and also as a safeguard both for the present and the future.

By 29 March Henderson had replied to Gee setting out a number of options to which Gee responded positively:

> For the present my wish is for myself and the Assembly here to become *associated* (Gee's emphasis) with the Elim work – as your second proposition. This could always lead to a complete merging of the work here with the Alliance – as your first proposition.

At this point, indeed on the same day, Gee decided to write to a fellow pastor, Ernest Boulton, who himself

had joined the Elim Alliance. This letter reveals some
of the personal soul-searching going on in Gee:

> I scarcely know what explanation to give you of
> my taking such a step in view of my past attitude
> . . . Old friendships are tugging very hard.

Gee then went on to justify his application by revealing
that:

> Three years in Scotland has been a hard school
> . . . I am persuaded that little will be done without
> some measure of organisation; and on making a
> personal visit to Ireland recently I found the
> Elim work as far as I could see, quite after my
> own heart.

Shortly after that letter it appears that George Jeffreys
came from Belfast, together with two companions, to
stay the weekend with Gee in Leith and to minister
to the assembly. Moreover during that weekend Gee
had crucial talks with Jeffreys about the legal aspect
of his approach to join the Elim Pentecostal Alliance,
especially the handing over of the property to the
Alliance Council.

Gee refers to these matters in a further letter written
to Henderson at Belfast Elim headquarters on 16 May
1923. He explains how a meeting of the assembly
trustees had taken place on the day following Jeffreys'
visit, and that all but one trustee had been in favour
of the transfer. Gee had then consulted the assembly
solicitor who had pointed out that under Scottish law
only a majority of trustees was required, not unanimity.
Therefore Gee with his usual business-like efficiency
goes on to say:

> I am enclosing for your perusal the trust deed for
> the property, and also the missive by which we
> hold the lease of the ground from the Caledonian

Railway Co ... Our solicitor suggested that if
you became a trustee for the property you could
probably secure a renewal of the lease, or a
fresh lease to yourselves on a more precise and
satisfactory terms.

The whole area of the transfer of trust deeds and
leases is crucial to an understanding of the fears of
many of the independent Pentecostal assemblies at
that time concerning Elim's organisation structure.
For an assembly to join the Elim Pentecostal Alliance
meant the surrendering of their property – a real loss
of independence and assets.

Two days after the above letter had been written
Gee, who had gone to London for the Whitsun Convention, sent a hurried handwritten letter to Henderson
explaining that the trustee who was against the Leith
assembly joining the Elim Pentecostal Alliance was
still quite adamant in his opposition despite some
initial signs of change. Gee was now anxious to inform
Henderson that there was 'not perfect unity regarding
Leith Assembly joining the Alliance'.

However, while Gee's application was being considered in Belfast a new issue was emerging which was
to have a pronounced effect upon the proceedings –
George Jeffreys had decided to revise the Constitution
of his Elim Pentecostal Alliance. In 1922 a rather loose
Constitution had been formed when Jeffreys' group
had adopted the official name of the 'Elim Pentecostal
Alliance'. Donald Gee had seen no major problems in
fitting in with this Constitution, as his letters already
show; but now in the middle of these important steps
Gee was informed by Henderson on 7 June 1923 that
the Constitution was under revision.

Initially Gee did not seem too anxious about the
revision, but when he received a proof copy of the *New
Constitution of the Elim Pentecostal Alliance* on 14 July
1923, he was greatly shocked by its implications. Gee

returned the proof copy on 18 July, together with a letter expressing his personal misgivings. He was never one to mince his words and in the opening paragraphs came straight to the point:

> After giving this Constitution a very prayerful and careful consideration it is with considerable disappointment that I feel unable to join the Alliance by signing the pledge to fulfil all obligations involved.

His first reservation was with the increased centralisation of powers and of Jeffreys' own personal position in all of this. The letter continued:

> I can quite appreciate that Pastor Jeffreys has found such success in the methods he has so far adopted that he feels abundantly justified in strengthening them in this manner: but for myself personally – much as I have come to see the value and legitimate place of organisation in the Church of God – I feel at present that this Constitution exceeds that which I am prepared to suscribe to.

It would seem that Gee secondly felt that the revised Constitution would restrict his own personal ministry, not leaving him free to choose when and where he should preach or exercise his much-demanded musical gifts. Part of Gee's reasons for applying to join Elim was to enlarge his scope of ministry, but now it would seem that Jeffreys might curtail his movements. Hence Gee's letter went on:

> Leaving on one side any question of principle as to the sovereignty of the Holy Spirit in the Church, I feel personally that I ought not to tie myself up to this extent. There comes to me occasionally, apart

from other ministries, opportunities of ministry on musical lines which I feel I must keep myself free to accept.

Finally Gee stressed that this decision did not at the moment affect the assembly at Leith or the transference of the property; on that issue he would be 'consulting with the trustees and leaders'.

Naturally the dramatic *volte-face* of Donald Gee came as a shock to the Elim leaders and within two days of Gee's letter they had replied with the compromise suggestion that 'the new Constitution could possibly be modified to suit individual cases'. However, Gee had made his decision and in all probability was relieved to be avoiding what was becoming an increasingly tangled situation. He replied to E.J. Phillips, the new General Secretary at the Elim headquarters in Belfast, re-affirming this previous decision:

I still feel after this further time for prayerful consideration that it it best for the time being for me not to join the Band.

Gee then went on to inform the Elim leadership that in his assembly the elders at Leith had further discussed the matter and that 'for the present the work should remain separate from the Elim Pentecostal Alliance and that no further steps be taken'. Moreover, Gee went on to ask for the return of the two legal documents which had been sent to Belfast, namely the trust deed and lease document relating to the property of the Leith assembly.

Thus quite dramatically and most unexpectedly the affair – almost a flirtation – with Elim was at an end. All the usual courtesies and niceties were observed – apologies for trouble and correspondence; an offer to defray expenses incurred and a looking forward 'to seeing you here again at some future time as the Lord

may lead'. But it was all finished and Gee's future lay
with the Assemblies of God.

Before we leave this interesting episode, it would
be useful to make a final assessment of it, especially
in terms of why Donald Gee made this surprising
application.

There appear to be three reasons why Donald Gee
wanted to join the Elim Pentecostal Alliance. First of
all, he was essentially a practical and organised man
and felt very conscious of the often ragged and ineffi-
cient nature of the independent Pentecostal assemblies.
The Elim movement offered to Gee a positive and practical way forward for his own ministry and assembly. A
second reason was that the Leith assembly was facing
serious financial problems, and there is no doubt that
to have handed over the property to Elim would have
been an enormous help and relief for Gee. Finally, there
were personal reasons for Gee's application. Gee felt
somewhat isolated in Scotland and saw the possibility
of his ministry stagnating. He considered the Elim
Alliance as a means of widening his own contribution
and opportunities. Early on in the negotiation with
Elim he commented to Henderson that he would 'be
equally willing to minister to any of the other Elim
Assemblies'. Thus it would seem that Gee was anxious
at that time to be developing and expanding his own
leadership role. Moreover, Gee appears ready to take
on a larger and less troubled assembly than Leith.
Although he somewhat sentimentalised the assembly
there in his book *Bonnington Toll*, it was a rather small
mission in the dockland area of Edinburgh and much
dominated by the patrons, the Beruldsen family. Gee
wrote to Phillips during his Elim negotiation:

Many things, and among them the greatly reduced
offerings, make me feel prepared to say (in confidence) that I rather expect the Lord will have work
for me soon elsewhere.

I do not think it would be unworthy to suggest that Gee's recognition of his own undoubted talents led him to feel that he could make a greater contribution by getting in at ground-level on George Jeffreys' ambitious expansion plans for Elim in England. Perhaps Gee revealed his true stature by refusing to continue with his application when he saw the principles at stake for his sense of independence and the price his own conscience would have to pay.

However, the Leith assembly did begin to prosper after this. The reason was in part Gee's involvement, not with an existing denomination, but in the forming of a new one – the Assemblies of God.

Chapter 5 – A New Denomination

For some five or six years during his time in Leith, Donald Gee was to be actively involved in the beginnings of the Assemblies of God movement in Britain. This was to be the denomination in which he was to hold high office throughout much of his life and which gave him accreditation for his wider international ministry. We shall be sketching first of all the events which led up to its formation and then asking questions about why such a movement was necessary and came into being. In and through it all, Donald Gee's part in these events will be seen and followed.

There were three main stages to the beginnings of the Assemblies of God in Britain – an abortive attempt at such an organisation at Sheffield in 1922 followed by a successful formation at Birmingham in 1924, together with a consolidatory conference in the same year held in London at the Highbury Missionary Rest Home belonging to Margaret Cantel.

The Sheffield conference had come about through a series of personal initiatives. William Burton, the outstanding Pentecostal missionary to Zaïre, had during his first furlough back in Britain during 1921 become aware of the lack of co-ordination among the independent Pentecostal assemblies. At the same time George Jeffreys, the Elim leader and evangelist, was preparing his strategy for expansion from Ireland into mainland Britain. He too saw the fragmented state of the various Pentecostal churches.

These two leaders, together with about a dozen other pastors, invited all the various leaders of the assemblies to meet with them for two days in the Montgomery Hall, Sheffield in May 1922. Jeffreys was conducting an evangelical mission in this hall at the time. About forty leaders attended the conference and some interesting details of it remain from the scribbled notes of Thomas Mundell, a solicitor and honorary secretary of the Pentecostal Missionary Union. Donald Gee was not able to be present, perhaps because of the distance involved, but he was certainly in support of what was happening, and significantly the conference passed a resolution to send personal greetings to Gee regretting his absence.

There appears to have been general agreement on the issue of forming a provisional council of the Assemblies of God in Britain, especially as about a dozen Welsh assemblies were negotiating with the recently formed American Assemblies of God about affiliating with them. However there does seem to have been fairly intense debate about the basis of faith for such an organisation, not the least on the issue of the initial evidence of speaking with tongues as a sign of baptism in the Holy Spirit. George Jeffreys seems to have spoken out quite strongly against the 'initial evidence' teaching.

However when the hundred or so Pentecostal assemblies were approached with this proposal for unity only about ten per cent were fully in favour and so the scheme was abandoned. It was apparent that some of the established leaders such as Cecil Polhill and Albert Saxby were against it and many of the ordinary pastors were suspicious of the centralised organisation associated already with George Jeffreys, fearing too much interference with their local autonomy. Moreover many of the assemblies were very protective of the long-standing emphasis among Pentecostals on the initial evidence of tongues – not the least as we shall

see later on, Donald Gee himself. At a personal level
the one man with the charisma capable of carrying the
scheme through the local churches, William Burton,
returned to Africa shortly after the conference and so
it failed to get off the ground.

Within two years of that failure, however, the Assemblies of God had been successfully launched. This was
because some newer younger leaders, such as Donald
Gee, were beginning to play a more active part. Another
factor was that the doctrinal emphasis was upon a more
thoroughgoing Pentecostalism; this struck the right
chord in the hearts and aspirations of the scattered
assemblies.

Although Donald Gee was part of the inaugural
planning group which met in Birmingham in 1924, the
real dynamic and organisational skill came from John
Nelson Parr, a Pentecostal pastor from Manchester of
similar age to Gee. Parr was a self-educated, capable
leader with strong gifts of communication and organisation. He had become a Christian in the holiness
movement but then had been baptised in the Holy
Spirit in 1910 after meeting with Christians who
had recently returned from Alexander Boddy's church
in Sunderland. By the mid-1920s he held a senior
management post in an engineering company as well
as pastoring the flourishing Bethshan Tabernacle in
Manchester.

It was this mixture of vision and business efficiency which caused him to bring together a small
group of Pentecostal leaders in February 1924 at
Birmingham and prepare a constitution acceptable
as a basis for the Assemblies of God movement in
Britain. Gee was present at Birmingham along with
some fourteen others, including Margaret Cantel. The
critical issue which seemed to carry the day over
all previous attempts was that there was to be no
centralised government of church affairs, but merely a
federation of independent churches meeting for mutual

encouragement and direction in local area presbyteries
and annually at a national assembly. Secondly the basis
of faith was strongly Pentecostal, with the doctrine of
initial evidence of tongues clearly included.

A few months later in May, Parr invited all the
assemblies to send representatives to a consolidatory
conference to be held in the Highbury Missionary Rest
Home in London. The purpose of the meeting was to
put the final touches to the constitution formulated at
Birmingham and to gain general approval of it. As a
result of this some seventy-four assemblies agreed to
form the Assemblies of God in Britain. This meant
that they formed the largest group of Pentecostal
churches in Britain and have remained so with some
500 churches today.

Although Donald Gee was involved in these plans
he nevertheless withheld his full involvement in the
new movement until October 1924, when his Leith
assembly became a member of the Assemblies of God.
He explained his reticence in a letter at the time, to a
colleague, Ernest Moser of the Pentecostal Missionary
Union:

> Twice already we have seriously and prayerfully
> faced the question at Leith of becoming united with
> some such organisation, and both times we have
> come to the conclusion that it was the will of the
> Lord for us to remain an entirely free assembly.

The two previous occasions Gee was referring to were
the Sheffield conference and his own personal approach
to the Elim Pentecostal Alliance.

One effect which Gee's hesitation did have was that
he was not eligible for election to the first Executive
Council of the Assemblies of God. However once Gee
had made up his mind about the new movement he was
quickly elected to leadership in 1925 and remained on
that body, even in an emeritus capacity, right up until

his death. However, had he been a member of that first
executive body, then his presence at a meeting in early
June 1924 might have made a radical difference to
the development and success of the whole Pentecostal
movement in Britain during later years. I am referring
to the dramatic approach by the Elim Pentecostal
Alliance to join in with the Assemblies of God.

On the first day of the Highbury conference in May
1924 a letter was read out to the delegates, signed by
three senior Elim leaders: George Jeffreys, Ernest J.
Phillips and Ernest Boulton. It read as follows:

It had been laid upon our hearts to send you a few
lines at the outset of your conference, which is,
we understand, being held at 73 Highbury, New
Park. Our purpose in writing is two-fold. First, to
contribute if possible to the uniting of the body
of Pentecostal believers in our land. Second, to
prevent (if the first is not successful) a breach
coming between yourselves as Assemblies of God
and the work of the Elim Pentecostal Alliance. In
view of what transpired at the Sheffield conference
two years ago, we fail to understand why nearly
all the Elim workers and assemblies have been
left uninvited to your deliberations. We contend
for the same truths, and believe that our aims
are one. The only possible difference between
us, is perhaps the interpretation of the elastic
term 'organisation'. We have read with interest your correspondence to the assemblies, and
the proposed constitution, the spirit of which we
appreciate. Is there any possible chance of us
getting together to talk over the matter of uniting
for the sake and glory of Christ? If any of you
consider that there are flaws or inconsistencies
in the work of the Alliance, why not have them
dealt with face to face in a Christian spirit? If there
is an opportunity of uniting instead of dividing,

surely we should avail ourselves of it in view of
our Lord's near return. If we fail to arrive at a
mutual agreement, then surely the attempt itself
will prevent us from drifting apart. If you consider
our coming together will achieve the purposes for
which we have written, we can arrange to meet
you at very short notice, as some of our workers
are at present in the city.

The outcome of this request was that the Elim leaders
were invited to attend the final day of the conference
and present their case to the delegation. On that day
Ernest Phillips made a dramatic plea that there should
be one united movement, with George Jeffreys and
his Elim group becoming the evangelistic arm of the
Assemblies of God.

There has been much speculation about why the
Elim delegation made their last-minute approach to
the Highbury conference. Obviously a powerful leader
such as George Jeffreys must have generally approved
of the action, but it could well have been Ernest Phillips
who saw the long-term advantages to Elim in such
a move. However, an interesting possibility is that
Donald Gee, who had already had close discussions
with Elim about joining them, still felt that there was
great evangelistic potential in having them on board
at the beginning of the new movement. Gee may well
have been the leader of a cautious pro-Elim movement
centred in the Highbury Missionary Rest Home itself,
where both Jeffreys and Gee were frequent visitors. He
may even have encouraged the Elim leaders to make
their approach to the conference.

This much at least can be gleaned from his later
history of the event, in which he wrote:

There had been strong hopes that Elim would
unite with 'Assemblies of God', and representatives of Elim visited the conference at Highbury

in May ... It should be understood that the difference between them is almost entirely one of church government ... This difference is more superficial than vital ... Such an issue need never become fundamental for Christian fellowship. (*Wind and Flame*)

However discussion of the issue was to take place at the first meeting of the newly elected Executive Council to meet in early June. As we have noted, Gee was unfortunately not yet on that body. It would seem that at that meeting although there was some encouragement from men such as John Nelson Parr, there were others who felt suspicious of George Jeffreys' autocratic approach to church affairs, especially Howard Carter, the influential principal of the Hampstead Pentecostal Bible School. Had Gee been present, he may well have swayed the meeting more decisively towards an evangelistic relationship with Elim.

However, Jeffreys shortly afterwards went on a visit to North America. There he saw first-hand some of the teething troubles of the American Assemblies of God. This caused him to write quite startlingly to Ernest Phillips in August:

The further I go in this Pentecostal Movement the more I am convinced that the democratic way of doing things is wrong. I am still persuaded that nothing will hinder me from going on with the Alliance as an independent work. Subject of course to the coming Band meeting. Don't have a single thing to do with them (i.e. Assemblies of God) until we can meet to discuss the whole situation.

When the Elim Evangelistic Band meeting took place in Belfast in December they arrived at the following decision:

> We, having beforehand carefully examined the
> minutes and prayerfully considered the question
> of amalgamation with the Assemblies of God of
> Great Britain and Ireland, believe it to be the will
> of God that we work each on our own lines . . .

Thus it would seem to have been the case, as Gee
noted, 'of strong personalities on both sides'. However
the speculation remains about the kind of dynamic
Pentecostal movement that could have been established in post-war Britain, had men of such calibre
as George Jeffreys, William Burton, John Nelson Parr,
Ernest Phillips and Donald Gee been active in the
one organisation. Perhaps Gee had just such a vision;
indeed, he was to write with great perception later on:

> A truly 'Pentecostal' Movement in the best sense
> of the word will always be pulsating with life, and
> will have within its borders room for a rich variety
> of expression of differing viewpoints, so long as
> there is the truly fundamental unity of the Spirit.
> (*Wind and Flame*)

Chapter 6 – Theological Struggles

As well as being involved in the process of the formation of the Assemblies of God, Donald Gee was also at the centre of the theological struggles and teaching which lay behind the need for such a movement. This particularly involved him in three issues: the debate about the initial evidence of speaking with tongues; the controversy with his former pastor Albert Saxby concerning the ultimate reconciliation of all mankind to God; and claims of the Pentecostal Apostolic Church about personal prophetic guidance. All of these matters were reasons why various Pentecostal leaders sought to form a united movement as a means of preserving a true Pentecostal testimony and protecting the independent assemblies from error and wrong practices.

It is well worth recounting these in a little more detail, for some of them are live issues today and the modern charismatic needs a historical backcloth against which to see his own understanding and teaching. He will often be surprised, too, at the importance and significance attributed to some of the issues in the early days of Pentecostalism and therefore will need to reflect carefully upon his own attitudes and perception today.

The 'initial evidence' issue

The topic of the initial evidence of speaking with tongues figured prominently in the early decades of

Pentecostalism and Donald Gee along with many others had much to say about it. The term 'initial evidence' is not a biblical one but came into common usage among early twentieth-century Pentecostal groups to emphasise the belief that everyone who was baptised in the Holy Spirit should speak with tongues as an evidence of that experience. For such groups, glossolalia became the only sign of a true Pentecostal experience. The biblical basis for this view was cumulative rather than directly expressed. As Gee wrote in *Redemption Tidings* in December 1925:

> The doctrine that speaking with other tongues is the initial evidence of the baptism in the Holy Spirit rests upon the accumulated evidence of the recorded cases in the book of Acts where this experience is received. Any doctrine on this point must necessarily be confined within these limits for its basis, for the New Testament contains no plain categorical statement anywhere as to what may be regarded as THE [Gee's capitals] sign.

The relevance of this doctrine to the issue of preservation of distinctive Pentecostalism as part of the reasons for the Assemblies of God being formed, becomes clear as Gee continues:

> Where they (Pentecostal groups) waver on this they usually become less and less recognisable as 'Pentecostal' churches.

Allied to this doctrine was the complementary teaching that the initial *sign* of tongues was distinct from the actual *gift* of tongues to be used at later times in the Pentecostalist's experience and worship. William Burton wrote:

> It must be made clear that though the believer magnifies God in tongues (Acts 2:11 and 10:

46), as the evidence, at that time, that he has received the Holy Spirit, he does not necessarily receive the gift of tongues, i.e. he may never have the ability to speak in tongues at will (1 Cor.14: 27) ... Speaking of the gifts, God asks, 'Do all speak with tongues?' (1 Cor 12:30). But on the other hand, 'The manifestation of the Spirit (as distinct from the gifts) is given to every man to profit withal' (1 Cor.12:7).

On another occasion Gee, having reiterated his belief in the 'initial evidence' went on:

I am not going to compromise, though I know that if there is one point where the teaching of Assemblies of God is going to become offensive, it is here.

Again, just before the negotiations to begin the Assemblies of God had started, Gee wrote an article in the *Elim Evangel* addressed 'To Seekers after the Baptism in the Holy Ghost'. In it he answered the question about how a person knows that he has received the Holy Spirit, and insisted there must be some positive manifestation.

What are the New Testament manifestations given with this experience? Several may be named; 'wind', 'fire', 'tongues', 'prophecy' etc.; the final choice of the Holy Spirit both then and now seems to rest on speaking in a new tongue. Why cavil at God's choice? ... God has chosen it for His sign, and rather we would simply accept it – humbly, cheerfully, adoringly.

There is little doubt that Gee was one of the most fervent

and eloquent apologists for this distinctive teaching. However the Carter brothers were also strongly committed to the view. Howard Carter in his book *Questions and Answers on Spiritual Gifts* asked:

> Would it be correct to say that the speaking with other tongues is actually the initial sign of Baptism in the Holy Ghost? Undoubtedly. On the Day of Pentecost they were all filled with the Holy Ghost and the evidence of their experience was that they spake with other tongues. It is clear by this that God intended us to recognize the reception of the Holy Ghost by this same manifestation of speaking with tongues.

In the preface to this book Carter mentions that his views on these topics originated during the period of World War I. This means that Carter's teaching on the 'initial evidence' would have been fully developed by the time of his involvement in the Birmingham Conference in 1924.

Similarly his brother John, his assistant at the Pentecostal Missionary Union Bible School at that time, held the same views. In a pamphlet on this topic he listed the occasions in the Acts of the Apostles where tongues and the receiving of the Spirit were linked, and then observed: 'A reasonable conclusion is that in all cases the initial evidence was the speaking with new tongues.' However, not all the Pentecostal leaders and groups held so rigidly to this doctrine. All placed value and importance on speaking with tongues, but not necessarily as the only sign of Spirit-baptism.

For example: on this issue, the position of the Pentecostal Missionary Union with regard to distinctive Pentecostal teaching was causing concern to some in the early 1920s. There is evidence that some of the Council were not prepared to endorse the idea of the 'initial evidence' of speaking with tongues. A fascinating account of a series of discussions relating to this subject exists in their Minutes for 1916. It appears that the Council were attempting to draw up a formal declaration on the controversial topic of the 'initial evidence'. On 23 May preliminary discussions took place leading to the following statement being passed as a basis for further debate:

The question of speaking in tongues in connection with the Baptism of the Holy Spirit having been considered, the Council expressed their unanimous opinion that whilst all who are now being so baptized do speak in Tongues, yet this is not the only evidence of this Baptism, but the recipient should also give clear proof by his life and 'magnify God'. Acts 10:46.

Ernest Moser was given the task of circulating this statement to the full Council. When the Council met again on 24 July it became clear that some kind of struggle was taking place to prevent a diluting of the 'initial evidence' teaching. The Minutes record the following observations:

Referring to Minute 5 of the Council Meeting held on the 23rd May last: The Formal Declaration referred to in the above Minute by Mr Moser (copy of which had been sent to each member of the Council) having been read and considered it was resolved that the Minute referred to be amended and read as follows: 'That the Council expresses their unanimous opinion that all who are baptized in the Holy Spirit may speak in Tongues as the Spirit giveth utterance, but the recipients should give clear proof of their life and "magnify God" Acts 10:46.'

It can be seen from this declaration that a compromise

position was reached, not ruling out the possibility of everyone speaking with tongues but certainly not suggesting that it was absolutely necessary. Moreover the added evidence of a holy life was also included as a sign of baptism in the Holy Spirit. Again it would seem that some of the Council members were not happy with this situation, notably Smith Wigglesworth who attended this second Council meeting, and most probably Moser. The reason for suggesting Moser as active in promoting a positive declaration in favour of the initial evidence is that he played a leading role in the formation of the Assemblies of God, which made this an article of its beliefs. Moreover from our knowledge of the way Moser often actively intrigued in the various causes that he held dear, it is interesting to note that despite the fact that Thomas Mundell was the Pentecostal Missionary Union Council Secretary it was Moser who circulated the statement to the members and surprisingly Smith Wigglesworth turned up at the next Council meeting. As Wigglesworth, generally speaking, strongly disliked committee meetings, it would be interesting to know what Moser said in the covering letters he sent to some of the members!

In the next Council meeting held on 7 November, a crucial turning point in the debate was reached. It seems that Wigglesworth, despite his dislike of committees, skilfully appealed to the growing unease of these Pentecostal assemblies who supported the Pentecostal Missionary Union with the ambiguous stance on the 'initial evidence'. The Minutes note:

> Mr Wigglesworth reported that the recent decisions of the Council as published in *Confidence* was considered very unsatisfactory by several of the Assemblies.

It was then decided to discuss the issue again at the next meeting.

The final meeting on this topic took place on 15 December and a complete reversal of the previous statements took place as the following declaration reveals:

The Members of the P.M.U. Council hold and teach that every believer should be baptised with the Holy Ghost and that the scriptures show that the apostles regarded the speaking with tongues as evidence that the believer had been so baptised.

Before leaving this intriguing episode some final observations need to be made. The question needs to be asked about who was encouraging the compromise position within the Pentecostal Missionary Union Council. It appears likely that this was Alexander Boddy, with Cecil Polhill being carried along by his views. Originally Boddy had personally held to the teaching of the 'initial evidence', mainly through the influence of T.B. Barrett, although it was not with the same dogmatic stance as many of the other Pentecostal leaders, as the following comment by Boddy reveals: 'For me Pentecost means the Baptism of the Holy Ghost with the sign of "Tongues". I dare not lay down any rule for others. I can only say this is the way the Lord led me.'

But it was at this time that Boddy came under the influence of Pastor Paul of Berlin and other German Pentecostals who were teaching a wider range of evidence for Spirit-baptism than just speaking with tongues. Boddy had met with them at a conference in Germany in 1910. Shortly afterwards he wrote:

The experience of these years of Pentecostal fellowship with many at home and abroad, fellowship with some of the Lord's best, has caused the writer to feel thus: He could not say of a stranger who came to him 'speaking in tongues', 'This man is baptised in the Holy Ghost because he speaks in tongues'. He would also have to see DIVINE LOVE (Boddy's capitals).

By 1914 Boddy's views had considerably hardened against the 'initial evidence' to the point where he wrote against it saying:

There is not one word of teaching to that effect in all the Scripture. Jesus, in the latter part of St John's Gospel, gave several evidences which would mark the coming and indwelling of the Holy Ghost.

Hence when we come to the Pentecostal Missionary Union debate about this issue in 1916 the compromise resolution of 24 July bears the stamp of Boddy. It is significant that at the meeting called on 5 December for a final decision on the matter after Wigglesworth had decisively intervened, Boddy was not present when the declaration in favour of the 'initial evidence' was accepted. He may well have diplomatically stayed away when he realised that his views were being rejected.

Further evidence that this issue was important is shown by the part it played in the Sheffield Conference of 1922 and the attitude of George Jeffreys and the Elim leadership. We have already seen how that the failure of the Sheffield initiative to secure an organisation of Pentecostal assemblies was partly the result of differences of opinion concerning the 'initial evidence' teaching. The personal notes of the Conference taken by Thomas Mundell reveal the debate on this topic.

Moreover the writings of some of the Elim leaders in the early 1920s show a similar view to that of Boddy which has just been described, that the evidence for Baptism in the Holy Spirit should be widened from just tongues to include signs of personal holiness. Ernest

Boulton writing in an official capacity within the Elim
Pentecostal Alliance as joint-editor of their magazine,
states:

> Whilst this initial outpouring of the Spirit was
> undoubtedly accompanied by various physical ma-
> nifestations, yet we should remember its chief
> purpose and most glorious outcome was profoundly
> spiritual. Care must be exercised to avoid focussing
> too much on the physical and relegating the
> spiritual to the background. After all it is the
> transformed life which provides the strongest
> argument as to the genuineness of any experience.

Similarly in an editorial in the following year Boulton
seeks to identify the genuine signs of the Pentecostal
experience. Nowhere does he mention speaking with
tongues but rather stresses that the baptism in the
Spirit is evidenced by an 'intensified love for Jesus
... a much more marked likeness to the Lord Jesus
... (and) a changed prayer life'.

From these examples about the significance of the
'initial evidence' of tongues it can be seen why many of
the leaders of the independent Pentecostal assemblies
felt that their distinctive testimony was being diluted
and that a new organisation of more fully Pentecostal
emphases was needed.

This was clearly revealed when the Birmingham
Conference held in 1924 formulated the *Fundamental
Truths* of the new Assemblies of God and firmly declared
its belief in: 'The baptism in the Holy Spirit, the initial
evidence of which is speaking with other tongues.' This
was a categorical and unambiguous statement setting
the British Assemblies of God apart from the previous
Sheffield initiative and from the Elim movement with
which they had many affinities. It was as Gee observed
the 'one point where the teaching of the Assemblies of

God is going to become offensive', but to those early pioneers of Pentecostalism it was an indisputable principle of their testimony.

In this particular stance the British Assemblies of God were following their American counterparts. Although Britain came under the influence of European Pentecostalism especially through Boddy's European contacts and conferences, there was a growing American influence as well, aided especially by the common language and growing literature. During 1918 the General Council of the American Assemblies of God had faced up to a major challenge on its own 'initial evidence' teaching. However, it firmly rebuffed the challenge and accepted the following resolution unanimously:

> That this Council considers it a serious disagreement with the Fundamentals for any minister among us to teach contrary to our distinctive testimony that the baptism in the Holy Spirit is regularly accompanied by the initial physical speaking in other tongues.

Before concluding this topic, it remains to be asked why Donald Gee and the early Assemblies of God leaders in Britain regarded the issue as so important.

The question is answered by Gee when he points out: 'It has been truly observed that, "It was the linking together of speaking with tongues and the baptism of the Holy Ghost that sparked off the Pentecostal Revival".'

Vinson Synan, commenting on the recognition of speaking in tongues as the initial evidence of Spirit-baptism made by Charles Parham in 1901, pertinently observes: 'It was precisely this settlement, that tongues were the only initial evidence of the reception of the Spirit, that gave Pentecostalism its greatest impetus' (*The Holiness-Pentecostal Movement*).

Thus what was at stake for many in this issue was not merely one theological point among others, but the most fundamental point of all, even affecting the true nature and survival of Pentecostalism. The British Assemblies of God did not just see itself as part of a movement forward into new territory but as being formed in order to maintain 'hallowed ground' and to allow nothing of its heritage to be lost. To deny the 'initial evidence' of speaking in tongues was tantamount to undermining the whole of the Pentecostal movement; and the British Assemblies of God was formed precisely to play a role in resisting that decline, at least in Britain.

Half a century later Gee was still adamant on this point. He wrote:

After over fifty years the smoke of battle has some-what cleared. Where are we now over this matter? Conservative evangelicals seem increasingly willing to have fellowship with us, and we are very happy to reciprocate in Christ. This does not mean that the other denominations have been converted to our particular doctrine, neither does it mean that we are prepared to compromise. What it does mean is that a clearer sense of proportion has come to us all. Donald Grey Barnhouse put it very neatly when he wrote that responsible Pentecostal leaders can now express ninety-five percent agreement with their fellow evangelicals, and within that large measure of hearty agreement there is ample room for fruitful fellowship in the things of God. But what about the remaining five percent? It is undeniable that this includes the testimony that speaking with tongues is the initial evidence of the baptism in the Holy Spirit. Should we surrender on that point? There is little doubt that the Pentecostal revival as a whole has no intention of doing so. Experience has proved that wherever there has been a weakening on this point fewer and fewer believers have in actual fact been baptized in the Holy Spirit and the testimony has tended to lose the fire that gave it birth and keeps it living. It may be claimed that evangelistic success has sometimes marked those who have modified their doctrine where 'tongues' are concerned. That may be so, and we rejoice in all ministries that bring men to Christ. But evangelistic success should not be our only criterion, although it is an easy and popular one. There is a fire of pure love and devotion to the Person of the Lord Jesus Christ that is the essence of the Pentecostal revival. There is a reality of the Holy Spirit in Pentecostal churches that meets a confessed lack in other circles. (*Towards Pentecostal Unity*)

It is not the intention or scope of this present book to give a theological critique of Pentecostal doctrine; a whole range of interpretive principles would need to be taken into account, not the least the validity of the Acts of the Apostles as normative for understanding such doctrines. However among Pentecostal teachers themselves there is no final consensus of opinion on the subject of the initial evidence of speaking in tongues. Michael Harper reveals something of the ambiguity of this topic among Pentecostals when he writes:

Many people ask the question: 'Must I speak with tongues when I am baptized in the Holy Spirit?' I would suggest that it is the wrong kind of question to ask. The answer is clearly – no. God will not make us speak in tongues if we are unwilling to do so . . . A better question to ask is: 'Can I speak in tongues when I am baptised in the Holy Spirit?' The answer to this question is gloriously – 'yes'. (*Power for the Body of Christ*)

What was important for the early leaders, such as Gee, was that experientially the initial evidence was true or correct for them and as such fulfilled their own understanding of a distinctive Pentecostal testimony. For other reasons, such as biblical exegesis, or the wider study of religion, such a view may be debatable; but for Gee and others it proved to be a determining factor in maintaining Pentecostalism as they saw it.

Early Pentecostal leaders did not develop a full theology of the significance of speaking in tongues; for example they did not explore its eschatological significance in terms of its relation to the coming of the Holy Spirit in the last days, nor its missiological significance in relation to the universality of the Spirit and the gospel. For pragmatic reasons they preferred to concentrate on the apologetic or practical significance of speaking in tongues, or at best, its theological relationship to the experience of the baptism in the Holy Spirit. Even today Pentecostals and charismatics have still not worked out the full implications of their doctrine of speaking in tongues and initial evidence. They increasingly face situations where many of their members have not spoken in tongues or have not experienced this phenomenon for a long period of time.

To sum up, Donald Gee was right to recognise the exceptional significance of the gift of tongues. It may not have been necessary for him to have insisted on it as the sole evidence of baptism in the Holy Spirit, but rather to rightly emphasise its importance and value. Surely that was the distinctive Pentecostal testimony which needed, and still needs, to be maintained. The teaching of the initial evidence of speaking in tongues overstates the case – but it does not underrate the significance of the gift.

The 'ultimate reconciliation' controversy

The next controversy to involve Gee seems to have

made its first public appearance as a serious issue at a Pentecostal leaders' conference held at Swanwick in 1921 when, says Gee, 'unhappy doctrinal issues clouded the spiritual sky'. By then Gee's former pastor Albert Saxby was beginning to openly articulate his views that eventually all would be saved by God; and some of the best-loved leaders in Pentecostalism were being affected by these views.

Saxby in 1923 in his own magazine *Things New and Old* took the opportunity to explain his opposition to the orthodox teaching on human destiny because, as he put it, 'some of our readers seem particularly nervous as to our views'. He stated that the orthodox view was based wrongly on:

    i.   The mistranslation of vital words in Scripture.

    ii   The refusal to take texts about God's universal grace literally.

    iii   The confusion of various ages and dispensations of God.

He concluded:

    'We do not believe there is any failure in the work of the Cross . . . Christ will see the travail of His soul and be SATISFIED [Saxby's capitals].'

At the same time he published various tracts and pamphlets supporting his teachings.

In one such pamphlet entitled *The Sheep and the Goats*, he sought to show that the sheep and goats were not 'the saved' and 'the unsaved', but 'different classes' of God's people. Both were 'clean animals' in the Old Testament law. The goats can never become sheep, but they do 'remain the property of the shepherd and he has a place for them'. In a further pamphlet Saxby sought to show how the term 'eternity' or 'eternal' frequently found in the Authorised Version and Revised Version of the Bible is best translated by 'age', and that the passages referring to 'eternal punishment' really only imply an 'age' or 'period' of punishment.

Replies to Saxby's teaching came from several quarters within the British Pentecostal Movement but the most eloquent came from Donald Gee in the form of an 'Open Letter' published in the *Elim Evangel* in 1924. Gee's leading part in this controversy stems from two causes. He obviously knew and admired Saxby and genuinely felt concerned for his former pastor. More important, Gee's own assembly and other Scottish assemblies were feeling the effects of this dispute. Gee had written to a colleague in London at that time:

> We are having a big fight here against Brother Saxby's doctrines of non-eternal punishment and universalism. The east of Scotland seems to be their stronghold. They have held a big Convention at Leith this weekend! Thank God, the assembly at Leith are standing firm with me for the truth, and more and more are expressing their gratitude for the stand we are taking. We are standing alone but the Lord is with us.

It was against that background that Gee published his 'Open Letter' to Saxby. He began by summarising the main views and biblical passages concerning human destiny. He then proceeded to stress the following principle: 'Truth is always reached by carefully balancing apparently conflicting statements.' Because there are texts supporting both sides of the argument the universalist reference must be 'modified' along two lines:

   i. By realising that God can be 'all in all' as much in justice as in mercy ... We must distinguish between final victory and final reconciliation – two quite distinct things.

   ii. By realising that the word 'all' must sometimes obviously be qualified.

Gee goes on to point out that the word 'all' in Scripture is not always used in a totally exclusive sense.

Next, the specific point of the translation of the word
'eternal' is taken up by Gee. Skilfully, he does not
attempt to be what he was not – a Greek scholar –
but resorts more to common-sense reasoning:

> I am compelled to say that I feel a criticism of the
> Authorised and Revised versions, and a flying to
> every other available translation to prove a point,
> strikes me as being one of the worst and weakest
> forms of argument ... The fact that a number
> of modern individual translations reject the word
> 'eternal' and substitute something less is to my
> mind significant, not of the faultiness of the older
> versions, but of the subtle tendency of this age of
> 'higher criticism' to whittle down and undermine
> all the fundamentals of evangelical belief, and all
> that is displeasing to the natural mind ... The
> Holy Spirit will be a safer Guide in the end than
> lexicons ... Have you ever gone to Him to enquire
> as to the true force of these words?

Gee continued his opposition to Saxby's views for several
years, writing strongly against them, and many other
Pentecostal teachers also campaigned against him.

A shrewd and not totally unsympathetic appraisal
of this controversy is given in some later observations
of Gee when he wrote:

> It seems fair now to suggest that Mr Saxby did not
> possess the theological training and ability to see
> through all the implications of his doctrine. Some
> have felt that had he been led more sympathetic-
> ally he could have been won to a more balanced
> position.

Nevertheless, Gee saw the dangers for the independent
assemblies and warned of 'the serious question of how
this (Saxby's teaching) affects our united front and

unity of heart as fellow-workers in the Master's service'. There is little doubt that this issue played a significant part in convincing the independent Pentecostal leaders, such as Gee, that the forming of the Assemblies of God was necessary.

The issue of 'prophetic guidance'

Finally the other issue in which Gee found himself caught up must be examined. This was a more widespread threat than that of 'ultimate reconciliation', although in practice it mainly affected the independent assemblies in South Wales. In essence it involved the rise of the early Pentecostal group known as the Apostolic Church, and their emphasis upon the role of apostles and prophets in matters of revelation and guidance for both churches and individuals. What brings added interest to this story is that the modern charismatic movement is seeing a resurgence of this type of Pentecostalism in some branches of the House Church fellowships; it is still very much a relevant issue today.

The beginnings of this movement were in South Wales, although closely linked with Bournemouth in southern England. Two Welsh mining brothers, Daniel P. Williams and William J. Williams from Penygroes in Carmarthenshire (Dyfed), were converted in the Welsh Revival of 1904 and then baptised in the Holy Spirit in 1907. The Pentecostal group to which they belonged showed a strong tendency towards guidance through prophecy. Soon Daniel, the leader of the two brothers, was pastoring the group and seeking to develop the whole role of prophetic ministry.

In parallel with these prophetic emphases in Wales a similar group had begun in Bournemouth, under the leadership of William O. Hutchinson. He had been converted in a Wesleyan Methodist church in 1881 but had later joined the Baptists. After spending several years in the Army reaching the rank of sergeant, he had left to take up a position in Bournemouth with the Society for the Prevention of Cruelty to Children. He had visited Boddy's Sunderland Conventions in 1908 and had been baptised in the Holy Spirit. This led him to begin his own Pentecostal assembly in Bournemouth, known as the Emmanuel Mission, Winton. Shortly afterwards in November 1908 he built the first-ever Pentecostal church in Britain; it was officially opened by Cecil Polhill. Hutchinson, like the Penygroes group, majored on prophetic guidance. Other assemblies joined him and their group became known as the Apostolic Faith Church.

Hutchinson's influence spread to Wales. Soon the Penygroes and other similar Apostolic assemblies were part of the Apostolic Faith Church. Under Hutchinson's prophetic direction, Daniel and William Williams were appointed apostle and prophet respectively among their Welsh assemblies. The group began to spread quite actively in the pre-war period. However, differences of opinion began to develop around Hutchinson's leadership of the movement. The outcome was that in 1915 the Penygroes group broke away from Hutchinson and formed itself into the Apostolic Church in 1916.

The group flourished and began to extend its network of influence throughout Britain by joining key centres to the movement. In 1919 the Burning Bush assembly in Glasgow joined them; in 1920 the Hereford assembly joined; lastly in 1922 the Bradford assembly linked with them. Together with Penygroes each of these centres acted as an administrative and missions centre for their respective geographical areas. The number of Apostolic assemblies grew from 50 in 1920, to 150 by 1930.

Whilst the Apostolic Church showed much in common with the other Pentecostal assemblies its distinctive feature in terms of teaching and practice lay in its insistence on using St Paul's description of church order

in Ephesians 4:11, as its model for church leadership:
the five offices of apostle, prophet, evangelist, pastor
and teacher should be recognised within the Pentecostal
Assemblies. Of course, it was the role of apostle and
prophet that was to prove most controversial; the other
offices were readily accepted by the other groups.

Apostleship was the senior office. The title should
be used and the apostle was to have chief authority
over church affairs. He was to direct the church either
by direct revelation or through the prophets within
his group. Once Hutchinson had designated himself
and Daniel Williams as apostles, then they in turn
were able by revelation to discern other apostles and
prophets to be appointed to office. Within the Apostolic
Church the leaders of the four key centres were the
only ones designated as apostles in the early years of
the movement.

The office of prophet was more widespread. It involved a direct revelatory function within the church and
was a governmental office, rather than one of general
worship or edification as in the other Pentecostal
groups. The prophets together with the apostles formed
the general councils of the Apostolic Church at local and
national levels. By means of prophetic direction deci-
sions would be taken about such matters as appointment of pastors, unveiling of doctrine, and controver-
sially, predicting the future for the benefit of the church
generally and the members of the church particularly.
Members would consult their local assembly prophet
on business and domestic matters. It was this aspect
of personal guidance – often known as 'consulting the
prophet' – that proved most controversial and divisive
in relations with other Pentecostal groups.

There is ample evidence that during the early 1920s
the Apostolic groups, with their prophetic practices
and proselytizing fervour among existing Pentecostal
assemblies, were causing growing concern and reaction.
William Burton wrote on the topic:

I find many people in these days are running
to so-called 'prophets' for instructions, and one
has seen most terrible blunders made by people
marrying, or investing funds, going on holiday,
or giving up situations and many similar things,
through advice and instruction given by tongues
and prophecy.

Burton goes on to suggest that it is not the gift of
prophecy that must be blamed, but the wrong use of
it. It is vital to prove and try all prophetic messages. He
went on to suggest that common sense forms part of this
judging of prophecy. If the prophetic word is directing
'square pegs into round holes', then reject it.

Donald Gee joined the fray against these Apostolic
practices, and in typical manner faced the issue squarely
by insisting on a biblical examination. He arrived at
several concluding principles concerning prophets and
prophecy after he had scrutinised the New Testament
evidence. He certainly wanted to encourage prophecy
within the church; but he went on to state that:

There is not one single instance in the whole of the
New Testament of 'enquiring of the Lord' through
a prophet ... There were always, apparently,
several prophets in each Assembly and they were
all on an equality with one another. Any such
office as 'set prophet' or 'anointed prophet' is
a sheer fabrication ... Lastly, the appointment
of persons to offices in the church through a
prophet is absolutely without any direct reference
or instance in the New Testament to support it.

He concluded with far-sighted wisdom:

The affixing of a label of office on a child of God
is not sufficient to equip with spiritual authority
and power.

In his history of the Pentecostal movement, Gee gives what is perhaps the best critique of the Apostolic Church:

> An attempt was made to institute a whole organised system of church government and ministry based on spiritual gifts. With this ideal we can have much sympathy. But one great cause of failure has always been the lack of distinguishing between mere names of scriptural offices, and the fact of the office in reality and power. To bestow New Testament titles of offices upon men and women, and then to consider that by so doing we are creating apostolic assemblies parallel to those of the Primitive Church, is very much like children playing at churches. It is the plain fact of the real spiritual gift and ministry within the individual that makes any office, and then the mere title is a secondary matter. (*Wind and Flame*)

It was in this school of practical experience that Donald Gee developed his teaching ministry and combined it with the writing and preaching skills which in his early days in Edinburgh he had sought to improve. These gifts, together with a credibility of his leadership within the new Assemblies of God movement, were to create wider opportunities within a short time for Gee. To these unfolding events we must now turn.

II. WIDENING MINISTRY

Chapter 7 – World Travels

Early in 1928 Gee received a surprising telegram at his Edinburgh home. It was an invitation to undertake a teaching tour of the Australian Pentecostal churches. Although Gee's old friends the Beruldsens had emigrated to Melbourne and had encouraged this invitation, there was nevertheless a growing overseas recognition of his teaching abilities through his magazine articles. Within a few weeks Gee had arranged a locum pastor, Ernest Mellor, for his own assembly and booked a passage on the 'Moldavia' sailing from Tilbury on 24 February. He was embarking on his first major overseas teaching tour and would be away until the end of the year, having visited five continents.

This was a significant moment for both Gee and the international Pentecostal movement. The main significance for Gee lay in the confirmation of his calling to a teaching rather than a pastoral ministry. Moreover, it was to introduce him to a much wider ministry than merely Britain. From now on his role was to be that of an international leader of Pentecostalism. Although he was to play an important part within the British Assemblies of God, he was to a great extent much more recognised and appreciated by the world-wide Pentecostal movement than he was within the British churches.

A further aspect of this lies in the realisation by Gee and a few other Pentecostal leaders that wise teaching and wise direction were badly needed within the growing Pentecostal movement. In his own reflections on the invitation to visit Australia, Gee noted with surprise:

> Moreover in those days such invitations to over-
> seas ministry only came to brilliant evangelists –
> who cared for mere 'teachers'? Their vital place
> in a Revival Movement was only dimly coming to
> be understood. *(Pentecostal Pilgrimage)*

An unusual confirmation of his vocation came in the
form of a dream. He had sold his car and divided the
money, some twenty pounds, between himself and his
wife Ruth, who remained in Scotland with the children,
for emergency expenses. Then he travelled by train to
London *en route* to join his ship. He stayed overnight
with his mother. Next morning he told her of a vivid
dream he had had in the night. He had dreamed he was
on board a large ship frantically stoking the furnaces,
until the ship was 'throbbing with fire and power'. Then
a fearful thought came to him that there may be no-one
on the bridge steering the vessel: 'In a frenzy of fear I
dropped my shovel, rushed up the iron ladders, on up
to the bridge and grasped the wheel only just in time
to swing the vessel off some rocks for which she was
heading at full speed.'

When he shared this experience with his mother at
breakfast she suggested that his coming voyage might
reveal the significance of his dream. Gee commented
later:

> It certainly did. In so many assemblies I found all
> the emphasis upon 'fire' and 'power' and hardly
> any importance being attached to wisdom and
> direction so that the 'power' was accomplishing
> something really useful for the glory of God. It
> was the Holy Spirit's own comfort and seal upon
> my particular ministry. *(Pentecostal Pilgrimage)*

Thus Gee's journey began full of excitement and anticipation carrying him forward into a new era of his life.

Although he would return to Scotland it would never be in the settled capacity of pastoral work, but rather his church in Leith being a base for a wider ministry.

Gee's leisurely voyage took him down through the Suez Canal and on into the Indian Ocean. However, he was not idle. He soon began to shape some of his church lecture-studies into book form; they were eventually to be published under the title *Concerning Spiritual Gifts*. This book was among his most influential writings and we shall look at in more detail later on.

When they docked for a short stay in Colombo, Gee managed to link up with some Pentecostal missionaries. However he was soon travelling again, reaching Australia at last. The ship arrived at first at Freemantle. Although his final destination was Melbourne, word of Gee's coming had gone ahead of him and he was quickly hauled off to speak at meetings in various ports *en route* – his fellow passengers were amazed at the number of friends he seemed to have in a land he had never visited before. But the highlight of his arrival was the reunion with the Beruldsen family in Melbourne. Their prayers and conversations brought back to Gee's memory the kindness of their first welcome in Edinburgh some eight years previously; now they were reunited for a while on the other side of the world.

Gee's main teaching ministry was in Richmond Temple in Melbourne, one of the largest Australian Pentecostal churches. It was led by Pastor C.L. Greenwood, an outstanding evangelist. He found himself having to adjust rapidly to a much less parochial situation than conservative Edinburgh – large congregations with choirs and orchestras were common in Melbourne. His main emphasis was to teach rather than evangelise, but one incident occurred which convinced Gee again of the truly Pentecostal nature and value of such teaching. He had preached on the subject of Jesus feeding the crowd of five thousand. Gee described what followed:

I was just concluding the sermon when the Spirit
of God fell upon one of the sisters sitting behind me
in the choir and she gave a remarkably appealing
message in tongues. The Holy Spirit very gra-
ciously gave me both to see and to speak the
interpretation. It was to the effect that the pierced
hands of Christ were gathering the broken, cast-off
fragments of humanity which men were trampling
under their feet and placing them in the baskets of
his eternal love and salvation. My own spirit was
profoundly moved as I seemed actually to see those
pierced hands at their glorious work. The effect
on the large congregation was deeply impressive
as men and women, without any further 'altar
call', began to move down to the front, both
from the floor and the gallery ... To me it has
always remained one of my most beautiful and
convincing experiences of the power and grace of
the gifts of the Spirit when exercised in divine
order. (*Pentecostal Pilgrimage*)

In September, Gee left Australia for a brief visit to
New Zealand. The great healing evangelist Smith
Wigglesworth had preceded him and Stephen Jeffreys
was to follow shortly. Again Gee's comments at that
time are perceptive; he remarked on the need for both
Australia and New Zealand to develop the more settled
ministries of pastors and teachers so that mature
growth could take place. Indeed the churches there
were beginning to recognise this and Gee had great
difficulty in refusing an offer from the New Zealand
assemblies to bring his family over from Scotland and
settle permanently among them. However, this would
have been a cul-de-sac for Gee's developing gifts and
ministry.

After leaving New Zealand he sailed to America
arriving in Los Angeles. An interesting experience for
him was to visit the Azusa Street Mission where the

twentieth-century Pentecostal movement had begun
in 1906. The building was still unchanged at that
time; Gee's photograph of it, frequently to be found
in Pentecostal histories, is one of the few survi-
ving pictures of that fascinating place. He then travelled through the Rocky Mountains by train and
across to the Assemblies of God headquarters at
Springfield, Missouri. Here he re-established contact
with Stanley Frodsham, the English biographer of
Smith Wigglesworth, at that time resident in America.
He also formed important links with the American
leaders Nelson Bell and Roswall Flower. Gee was
held in high regard by the American assemblies and
became something of a cult figure through his regular
visits and books. It was on this first visit to Springfield
that he negotiated with the Gospel Publishing House
the publication of *Concerning Spiritual Gifts*, his first
book. They were to continue to be his main publishers.
Finally he went up into Canada to establish links with
the Canadian Pentecostal leader Robert McAlister
before returning to his home in Edinburgh in time
for a family Christmas and the New Year convention
with his church in Bonnington Toll.

The next few years were among the most significant
for Gee's international contacts as he continued to
travel widely. 1929 saw him back again in America
having his first taste of ministry at the distinctive
Camp Meetings and attending the General Council of
Assemblies of God. He was given an open door to all the
business sessions and gained an important insight into
how the American Christians ran their church affairs.
Gee witnessed the election of Ernest S. Williams to the
position of General Superintendent – the most powerful
Pentecostal office in the world – a post Williams was to
hold for some twenty years. Such contacts were decisive
for Gee's future career and ministry.

If Williams was influential in America, then Lewi
Pethrus the Swedish Pentecostal leader held similar

sway in Europe. In the following year, Gee was invited to visit Scandinavian churches where he re-established his brief earlier links with Pethrus at the impressive 'Filadelphia' Pentecostal church in Stockholm which, with some 6,000 members, was the largest Pentecostal church in the world between the two world wars.

From there Gee visited Finland and then finally met up with Thomas Barrett, the veteran Norwegian Pentecostal leader, in Oslo. It was Barrett who had first introduced the Pentecostal message to Alexander Boddy in Sunderland back in 1907. On nearly all of these visits Gee was teaching his congregations about the gifts of the Holy Spirit as described in his book on that subject. Everywhere he went he found a great hunger for such careful and balanced biblical exposition.

In 1931 Gee made his first trip to eastern Europe. He taught in the Danzig Bible School and then journeyed on into south-west Russia. Pentecostal believers packed the wooden halls and the meetings often lasted for as much as four hours. Here there was little of the glamour of Gee's previous travels. Much of the transport was by horse and cart over what appeared to be endless frozen marshland. Often at night he would sleep in the same room as the men of the farm and the women would sleep in the cow-barn; washing would be performed outside with a simple bowl of water. Nevertheless Gee was gaining an insight into the Pentecostal movement which few others had. When he returned home, the *Edinburgh Evening News* was happy to publish his account of this remarkable visit.

Finally in 1932 Gee travelled extensively in the Middle East, especially Palestine. In characteristically abrasive style he warned against an over-sentimental approach to visits to the Holy Land and against the over-enthusiasm of prophetic teachers. He commented later on:

> Speaking for myself I can only say that I hardly
> ever felt our Lord's presence less than when tra-
> versing the scenes of his earthly life and ministry.
> He is with us now by his Spirit wherever we may
> be on this earth. *(Pentecostal Pilgrimage)*

However he did concede that Bible teachers gained
further understanding of the outward setting of the
Scriptures by such visits. So presumably Gee himself
had been helped by his own visit.

It was becoming obvious that Gee was only the pastor
of his Edinburgh assembly by name, since he was away
so frequently. Even Ruth his wife was away with him
on some of the visits. Hence in 1933 they decided
to move to Louth in Lincolnshire where Ruth would
have a role as matron of the Pentecostal Women's
Bible School organised by Howard Carter, who himself
was principal of the men's college in Hampstead, north
London. Donald would be free to travel. This was an
amicable arrangement and the Edinburgh assembly
were sad to see them go. They wrote the following
tribute to Gee in the official magazine of the Assemblies
of God:

> Our assembly has been completely changed since
> he came and the same influence which wrought so
> much good in our own assembly was felt through-
> out all the assemblies in Scotland . . . A beautiful
> model of a Remington portable typewriter was
> presented as a token of esteem . . . We are only
> happy in the knowledge that God has thrust him
> forth from us to a much wider field. (*Redemption
> Tidings*, April 1933)

Ruth and Donald Gee stayed in Westgate House, Louth,
for the whole of the Second World War and then moved
to Bedford. Meanwhile Ruth's health had been causing

concern. She eventually died in 1950 while Donald was away in Belfast.

He had continued his itinerant ministry before the interruption of the war, visiting South Africa, and, more importantly in 1937, Japan, China and Korea. His last pre-war venture was to share with Lewi Pethrus in organising the European Pentecostal Conference held in Stockholm in 1939. Gee was to become a widower, almost sixty years old. But his career was to take on new directions though with the underlying stability of working in a settled base in England. The new directions were to involve his appointment, at the 1947 World Pentecostal Conference in Zurich, as the first editor of the new international magazine *World Pentecost*. Secondly, in 1951 the British Assemblies of God united two smaller Bible colleges to create one main college at Kenley in Surrey; Donald Gee was invited to become the first principal.

More of that story later; for the present it will be helpful to try to assess something of the significance of those important travelling years. We will then evaluate the books and teaching which emerged through Gee during that period.

For Gee himself the early travel years of the 1930s were somewhat akin to the apostle Paul's years in Arabia. They enabled him to stand back and look at the Pentecostal movement as a whole. Thus they were important grounding years for his future international ministry, and especially the overview required for the editorial ministry of *World Pentecost*.

At another personal level they were the years when he developed his so-called 'ministry of balance'. Gee in his later years was nicknamed the 'apostle of balance'. It all went back to that first dream he had had of the ship needing steering as well as powering. His experience and knowledge of many churches in a wide range of countries led him to feel early on that his ministry and teaching must try to offset and correct some of the extravagance and fanaticism which he observed in parts of Pentecostalism. He spoke of rescuing the Pentecostal movement from its friends as well as its foes. Something Gee found most disturbing was meetings dominated by chorus singing and speaking with tongues, yet with very little encouragement to biblical preaching and teaching. Similarly, he felt that an almost total emphasis on healing, especially in large evangelistic meetings, was obscuring both true evangelism and Pentecostalism as a wide-ranging experience of the Holy Spirit.

Yet this emphasis on balance must not be seen as diminishing Gee's concern for a full-orbed life in the Spirit. He wrote later on about his earlier dream of the ship:

It would be equally futile, if not equally dangerous, if all the attention on the ship was on the bridge and none in the furnaces. For the fire to go out or even to die down, is for the power to cease. The vessel would become stationary. It might even become ice-bound! Unless the engines are throbbing with power and the vessel is forging ahead, there is nothing to steer. Vessels in dry dock need no navigating. There is nothing for teachers to do unless their evangelistic brethren are fulfilling their gifted ministry and our prophets are stirring our hearts with burning messages from on high. To be Pentecostal we must all have the holy fire. (John Carter: *Donald Gee – Pentecostal Statesman*)

All of this sometimes led to misunderstanding and criticism of Gee by some of his fellow Pentecostalists, not least in Britain. Gee could get away with his abrasive observations – made in his rich, slightly growling, voice – in foreign countries. But in his native Britain he was not always so well received. He

was often regarded as bullying or pompous. Added to
this may well have been a touch of envy among some of
the other leaders over the opportunities Gee had and the
popularity he generated in the world-wide Pentecostal
movement. A prophet is not without honour except in
his own country.

Similarly Gee's frequent journeys seemed to isolate
him from his family, especially his children. They were
brought up in their formative years almost solely by
their mother, particularly in the period at Louth.
Donald would on occasion take Ruth with him abroad,
but this was only possible on rare occasions because
the children needed to be looked after at home. Nevertheless Gee seems to have had a happy marriage. After
Ruth's death he seemed to be a rather lonely figure.
It was more his austere and shy personality that led
to his lack of close communication with his children,
rather than his absence. His children did not appear
to suffer from this, going on to make successful careers
for themselves. Winifred became a teacher. David,
after gaining a theological degree, went into pastoral
ministry. The youngest daughter, Olive, was the most
intellectually gifted of all; having achieved a doctorate
in history she went on to lecture in higher education.

The significance of Gee's itinerant ministry for the
Pentecostal churches as a whole can be summed up
by some of his own assessments. Such travels, he
said, did much 'to establish Scriptural principle among
Pentecostal people that the gifts of Christ to the church
(Ephesians 4 verse 11) are set in the whole body and not
locally in one assembly' (*Wind and Flame*). Towards the
end of his life he made his most perceptive comments
about these formative travel years:

> It entailed pioneering a new type of ministry to
> be designated 'Pentecostal'. Up till then world-
> travellers in the movement had been almost exclu-
> sively healing-evangelists. The discovery that the

opening of the scriptures by the Spirit of Christ can still yield burning hearts was a thrill to tens of thousands. Undoubtedly it was sound teaching on ALL [Gee's capitals] the gifts of the Spirit that constituted the key-note and the key. It met a clamant need. Doors sprang open everywhere. There was no seeking for invitations, the problem was to meet those that poured in. (*Bonnington Toll*)

The decade of the 1930s was the period in which Gee embodied much of his teaching into book form. We can now go on to look at some of these writings, and attempt to find out what made him such a sought-after teacher.

Chapter 8 – Ministry Gifts

Donald Gee was a prolific writer. He produced some twenty books and countless articles for various Pentecostal magazines. His most important books were written in the period before the Second World War and came out of his itinerant teaching ministry. Hence most of his writings were of a pastoral teaching nature, with a second important strand – Pentecostal history – developing towards the end of that period.

Within the first area, pastoral teaching, two main categories of material can be distinguished: Pentecostal doctrine, and practical Pentecostal conduct or living.

Gee's first love was Pentecostal doctrine, so major books on the subject appeared early in his writing career. *Concerning Spiritual Gifts* was published in 1928 by the American Assemblies of God. It contained Gee's own clear understanding of the nine Pentecostal gifts of the Holy Spirit as he found them in 1 Corinthians 12: 8–10. This was followed shortly afterwards in 1930 by what Gee described as the sequel to his earlier book on gifts. It was entitled *The Ministry-Gifts of Christ*. Gee sought to describe the five ministries of apostle, prophet, evangelist, pastor and teacher as indicated in Ephesians 4:11. Some general observations on the skill and value of Gee as a teacher can be made from these formative books, before we examine them in a little more detail.

Firstly, a key interpretive feature of Gee's Pentecostal teaching was his emphasis on the relationship

between gifts and ministries as a means of understanding the true significance of both. He wrote:

> The close relationship between the various particu-
> lar gifts of the Spirit and the various offices or
> ministries set by God in His Church is made very
> apparent by their juxtaposition in 1 Corinthians
> 12 (compare verses 8–10 with verse 28). The one
> subject logically arises from the other; indeed they
> are not even different subjects, but only two aspects
> of one and the same. (*Concerning Spiritual Gifts*)

Gee was always concerned to earth the supernatural
gifts into recognised ministries and never to see the
gifts of the Spirit merely as an end in themselves.

> The whole subject of spiritual gifts must be finally
> related to the realities of the world in which the
> church is called to work and witness. (*Concerning
> Spiritual Gifts*)

It was in the work of evangelism outside, and the
development of a mature church life within, that Gee
saw the most significant contribution of spiritual
gifts. He challenged any notion that cosy-huddles or
élitism were part of true Pentecostalism.

This refusal to treat spiritual gifts in isolation
contrasts in a most valuable way with some other
Pentecostal teaching on the gifts of the Spirit which
gave the impression that every Christian could anticipate exercising any of the gifts, whatever may be their
role in the church. Of course Gee was not in favour of a
one-man ministry approach, but he saw the dangers of
an indiscriminate encouragement to seek for gifts. He
concluded:

> The ideal, and scriptural model, is a perfect blend-
> ing of liberty for *all* [Gee's italics] to share in

spiritual ministry, with a recognition that *some*
are divinely appointed to offices of leadership
and divinely gifted for outstanding ministries . . .
(*Concerning Spiritual Gifts*)

Gee developed this idea with the helpful insight that
'spiritual gifts are in the church rather than in the
individual'. He encouraged his readers to pray for
ministries that they might use in the church rather
than merely individual gifts. Such ministries would
then need the complementary gifts of the Spirit to
make them effective. This blended in with Gee's views
on the overall purpose of the baptism of the Holy Spirit,
which he believed to be power for service in the whole of
church life. For Gee, Pentecost meant gifts-in-ministry.
This emphasis, if Gee is correct, provides a helpful
contribution to the modern charismatic debate, as one
sees that an experience quite distinct from conversion
or holiness, but more relating to service in the church,
is a meaningful understanding of the purpose of being
baptised in the Holy Spirit.

As we will see, this approach led Gee to make some
radical reappraisals of the meaning of certain gifts of
the Spirit, especially the linking of the word of knowledge with a teaching ministry. In 1963 he was invited to
be guest lecturer at LIFE Bible College in Los Angeles.
These lectures contain his most developed ideas on
relating spiritual gifts to ministry gifts. The lectures
were published later on, under the title *Spiritual Gifts
in the Work of the Ministry Today*. A further general
point relating to the linking of ministries and gifts is
that although Gee took a fairly practical attitude to
gifts he never lost sight of or devalued the supernatural
aspect of either gift or ministry.

The purely natural abilities and characteristics
of the believer may provide a background upon

which the Holy Spirit works with His supernatural gift; and indeed, this is never more clearly instanced than in the personalities used by Him for the writing of the inspired Scriptures. But the ministry-gift is something added by the Holy Spirit. (*The Ministry-Gifts of Christ*)

This in turn led Gee to make challenging statements about the whole concept of ministry. He urged:

The great principle to stand for concerning the ministry is that it must be based on spiritual gifts ... We must not let ourselves be misled by mere labels of office. True ministry-gifts consist not in the name but in the power. (*The Ministry-Gifts of Christ*)

Similarly he observed:

Having established the principle that all true Christian ministry springs from a divine equipment, it is well to pause for a moment to measure how far we have wandered from this principle today when men are accepted for the work of the ministry who do not even have any real witness to the new birth, let alone that baptism in the Holy Spirit which is the first great essential for effective service. And added to this, the average training given is simply a packing in of purely natural knowledge and the improvement of purely natural endowments, with practically no regard for spiritual gifts. (*Concerning Spiritual Gifts*)

However Gee never subscribed to the view that the gifts were so supernatural as to be almost unrelated to the recipients' natural gifts and personality. He admitted that it was difficult 'to try and discover the exact point where the supernatural is added' and that 'there are some ministries that on the surface appear to have less of the supernatural about them than others'; rather he felt that we should 'enlarge our conception of that truly supernatural life'. He concluded: 'To see the Holy Spirit at work where we have not done so before, can be an exciting and enriching advance in our personal life.' (*Spiritual Gifts in the Work of the Ministry Today*)

A final comment needs to be made on Gee's style and approach. He makes no claim to being an academic theologian and so his material is free from technical jargon or the 'quote and counter-quote' method of some theological books. However, he writes from deep personal conviction and a wide experience of Pentecostal issues. His books are extremely readable, written in his characteristic flowing prose, full of salty phrases and helpful illustrations. The overriding impression of his books is that they are biblical and practical.

Although Gee's first book was on spiritual gifts, it will be helpful to look initially at its sequel on the subject of ministry-gifts, for as we have seen, Gee anchored his teaching on gifts in ministries.

He identifies five main ministry-gifts, although he includes also some minor ones such as 'helps' and 'exhorters'. Gee seems to have clearly held to the view that Christians are given divine ministries, quite distinct from mere human abilities – and that these roles are enhanced and validated by corresponding spiritual gifts. He also firmly believed that these ministries existed in the twentieth-century Pentecostal church, although he felt that some of them were scarcer than some groups claimed. His guarded warning was that ministry-gifts should be recognised or self-evident, rather than created by a church-appointments board.

The ministry-gift of being an apostle was the most significant and far-reaching. Gee felt that such a ministry combined virtually all the other ministries of prophet, evangelist, pastor and teacher as well.

Its distinctive work was that it was foundational in the sense of church-planting and formative strategy and more widespread than the limitations of a local area ministry. Gee saw the apostle as exercising an authoritative leadership not dissimilar from the later role of bishops. Just as the apostles combined a whole range of other ministries in their one ministry-gift, so, in Gee's teaching, they above all would be most likely to exercise the greatest range of spiritual gifts to fulfil their ministry effectively. When searching for modern examples of such apostles, Gee suggests that they are more likely to be found among the missionary pioneers and leaders. He comments cautiously:

> It is not easy to find the type of man who we feel has a just claim to be considered an 'apostle' in the scriptural sense. The most likely field will undoubtedly be among our missionaries, for the very nature of their work demands and calls forth at least something of the ministry of an apostle. (*The Ministry-Gifts of Christ*)

It is well known that Gee thought highly of the remarkable pioneering work undertaken in Zaire from 1915 onwards by William Burton and his companions. In his later historical writings Gee refers to this ministry in terms of 'truly apostolic labours'; perhaps Burton was one such man whom Gee had in mind when seeking to identify the modern apostle.

When he came to discuss the ministry-gift of prophet, Gee made some helpful preliminary observations. Although he recognised that a prophet exercised some kind of preaching ministry, he clearly refuted the popular non-Pentecostal teaching that in the New Testament, prophecy and preaching were the same activity. As we shall see, for Gee prophecy was preaching with a plus. He also pointed out that there is a distinction between the spiritual gift of prophecy

and the ministry-gift of prophet. Gee is surely right
to emphasise the major role that the office of prophet
played in the New Testament, being second only to
that of the apostle, whereas the gift of prophecy at
the popular level of 'strengthening, encouragement
and comfort' (1 Corinthians 14:3) seems to have been
widespread in the church. Lastly Gee was concerned
that the prophet should not be seen as some kind of
fortune-teller, merely involved with personal guidance.
Here he is reacting against some of the early Pentecostal
groups who appointed 'set prophets' in each assembly
and their guidance was sought for a whole range of
local and personal matters.

Gee's main emphasis in interpreting the work of the
prophet is to stress an intuitive and revelatory role
linked closely to the major directions and strategies
of the church, for example the missionary initiative
of the church at Antioch (Acts 13: 1–3). They were
people acutely 'sensitive to the spiritual atmosphere'
around them. He suggests that the main vehicle for
communication used by the prophet was preaching,
but more inspirational than carefully prepared. They
would be sensitive to what God was wanting to say
and do, hence the spiritual gifts most likely to be
found among them would be the revelatory gifts of
wisdom, knowledge and discernment, coupled with
acts of supernatural faith.

The ministry-gift of the evangelist is easier to identify, but Gee along with other Pentecostal leaders was
in the thick of the 'signs and wonders' debate long
before John Wimber appeared on the scene. Gee was
quite emphatic that the spiritual gifts of healing and
miracles were a necessary part of the evangelist's
ministry, especially to authenticate and advertise the
gospel. He remarks:

The principle also stands strikingly revealed that
a display of divine power and blessing upon any

ministry is the very finest form of advertising. No
fleshly, worldly flourishing of trumpets can ever
take its place if we want revival in the power of
the Holy Spirit. There is a place for legitimate
publicity, but we have seen advertising 'stunts'
in evangelistic work which are nauseating and
can only result in completely grieving the Spirit
away. Divine power soon draws crowds. (*The
Ministry-Gifts of Christ*)

Gee was closely associated with the evangelistic ministries of such men as Smith Wigglesworth and Stephen
Jeffreys, both of whom conducted missions in Gee's
assembly in Edinburgh. Hence he based his views on
those experiences. Nevertheless his importance as a
leading teacher in those early days of the Pentecostal
movement is revealed by some of the pertinent comments which he made about evangelism. He rightly
pointed out that 'miracles arrest and compel attention,
but it is the preaching of the Word that converts and
saves.' He noted: 'True evangelism must "preach the
Word" as its central and essential factor, whatever
place may be given to personal testimony, healing
or other legitimate features.' (*The Ministry-Gifts of
Christ*)

Another concern of Gee was that the healing evangelists were virtually taking over the Pentecostal movement. This created various problems which he felt
needed to be countered. One was the need to appreciate
other ministries such as church-planting and teaching,
which must not be devalued by an over-emphasis on
evangelism. Another was that healing evangelism was
being seen almost as the sum total of the Pentecostal
experience – healing was virtually replacing the baptism of the Spirit as an experience in its own right. This
meant that some of the new assemblies being formed
were scarcely recognisable as being truly Pentecostal.
Finally Gee was quite realistic in recognising that in

many healing crusades only a small number of definite
healings appeared to happen, and of the vast numbers
of people professing conversion sometimes only rela-
tively few remained to be part of the local church.

Despite these reservations Gee still insisted on the
importance for the Pentecostal churches of recognising
the ministry-gift of the evangelist. 'The permanent
results of the great campaigns have been impressive
enough,' he concluded, 'even when every discount has
been allowed.'

Gee treated the pastoral gift more straightforwardly,
linking it as we shall see with the gift of prophecy and
discerning of spirits, but he interpreted the ministry-
gift of teaching in a unique manner. Gee, of course,
throughout his ministerial career had been wrestling
with his own problems of self-identity within the
Pentecostal movement. He recognised that he was not
called to be a pioneer missionary. In his very early years
as a Christian he was almost terrified by the thought of
being called to work overseas, although he writes later
of overcoming that fear. Similarly he knew that evangelism and healing crusades were not his gift, which
was much more that of teaching. His Pentecostal convictions and his desire not to be overshadowed by those
more spectacular ministries led him to see the ministry-
gift of teaching as being as much a supernatural endow-
ment as the other offices. This was because, in his view,
teaching was directly related to the spiritual gift of a
word or message of knowledge (1 Corinthians 12:8).

This distinctive view is found in the earlier editions
of his book *Concerning Spiritual Gifts*, but it was most
fully set out in an addendum to that book in 1947.
In that extra note Gee sets out three reasons why
he believes that a word of knowledge is linked with
a teaching gift in the church. First of all he reminds
us of his basic axiom that *spiritual gifts must be
understood in terms of ministry-gifts* and that the
whole context of Paul's discussion of spiritual gifts in 1

Corinthians 12–14 is that of corporate church meetings
and ministry. Among such channels of ministry to the
church is listed 'doctrine' or 'a word of instruction' (1
Corinthians 14: 26). He concludes: 'If doctrine, which is
a ministry of teaching, is connected with any gift of the
Spirit referred to in chapter 12 verses 8–10, it will be
either the word of wisdom or the word of knowledge, and
most simply the latter.' (*Concerning Spiritual Gifts*)

He develops this conclusion with his second point:
that *teaching and knowledge are obviously linked
together*. Knowledge imparted by God will 'make a
man a teacher as nothing else will do'. Gee suggests
that such knowledge comes about when revelation,
meditation and instruction are fused together by the
Holy Spirit.

The third reason Gee puts forward is that the *'highly
important office of teacher within the church does
require to be linked up with some recognised manifestation of the Holy Spirit'*. He notes how prophets
and teachers were linked together in ministry (cf Acts
of the Apostles 13: 1–3), and that it is unlikely that
one would involve purely natural abilities and the other
supernatural.

Gee, of course, is on easier ground when he is stating
these inner convictions concerning a role which he felt
was often devalued among Pentecostal churches, than
when he comes to say more exactly what such words
of knowledge are in fact and practice. He concedes that
much good teaching goes on in church life as the result
of natural academic abilities, but there are occasions
when the Holy Spirit is more significantly at work.

There come times when the Spirit of revelation
is so operating through a teacher exercising an
anointed ministry that we become conscious of
an illumination transcending all natural ability
either to gain or to impart . . . We know it because
our hearts burn within us as surely as theirs

did on the Emmaus road when the risen Christ
'expounded unto them in all the Scriptures the
things concerning himself.' By the gifts of the
Spirit that Voice still expounds the scriptures on
that sweetest of all themes – 'himself'. (*Concerning Spiritual Gifts*)

Gee further stated that all the original insights of the
New Testament writers, especially in the doctrinal
passages, were in this category of words of knowledge imparted through inspired teachers. Thereafter
the ministry of teaching was to receive interpretive
insights through the Holy Spirit in terms of both
understanding and practising the New Testament.
Gee particularly applied this to the whole area of
distinctively Pentecostal doctrine which he and others were seeking to expound in those early days of
the Pentecostal movement. Moreover, he regarded
the audience's response as an integral part of any
exercise of an authentic ministry-gift of teaching. To
Gee it was only when the Holy Spirit moved among
the congregation and caused it to respond that the
natural gift of teaching could be distinguished from
the supernatural. The occasion in Australia that has
already been described, when Gee's teaching sermon
was further elaborated as he interpreted a message in
tongues and many of the congregation spontaneously
began to walk to the front of the church seeking
repentance and help, best illustrates this view.

As can be seen, this is an exhilarating understanding of such a Pentecostal ministry of teaching. Gee
bemoaned the kind of assembly that only thought that
a meeting was truly Pentecostal when someone had
been healed or had spoken in tongues. However, he
observed:

All this is corrected and brought into true perspective when we see that in an anointed and inspired

ministry by one of Christ's teachers set within
the church we have been listening to the 'word
of knowledge' as a gift of the Spirit. (*Concerning
Spiritual Gifts*)

Gee's distinctive views on this subject cut right across
the popular teaching of his day and that of many
modern charismatics: that a word of knowledge is some
supernatural revelation of a person's sickness, need or
situation. Indeed, it is fair to point out that Gee's views
about the word of knowledge were not widely accepted
within the Pentecostal movement. Nevertheless his
writings on this subject have stimulated debate concerning it, and they rightly challenge what often seems
to be on the one hand a reduction of the spiritual gift of
a word of knowledge to mere personal words of insight
and direction, and on the other hand, the undervaluing
of the ministry-gift of the teacher to a purely natural
talent of instruction.

This emphasis by Gee was to prove an uphill struggle
throughout his whole teaching career. Nevertheless he
manfully held to his views and continued to develop
them. Even as his ministry was drawing to a close he
challenged the students in his lectures at LIFE Bible
College in the following manner:

The climate of the early decades of the Movement
gave scant encouragement to a teaching type of
ministry. All the emphasis was on evangelism, and
that of a rather garish type. If the holy scriptures
were quoted it was rather to support experience
than instruct it. It has to be ruefully admitted
that teachers, as such, often undermined their
own acceptance because they brought over into the
Pentecostal Revival the methods they had used in
their former denominational churches. Their ministry therefore seemed to present a descent into the
natural from the supernatural that accorded ill

with the essence of the Pentecostal Revival. There
was much truth in this complaint, and teaching
by natural gifts laid a foundation for that wrong
conception of the basically spiritual gifts that are
at the root of a truly Pentecostal ministry of the
Word. Any realization that a teaching ministry
could be as truly 'Pentecostal' as healings or
miracles was difficult to fit into the prevailing
emphasis on the apparently supernatural at all
costs. It shall be an important part of our business
in the course of these studies, if God permits, to
present a truer picture of the proper nature of
teaching and teachers within a spiritually gifted
church. This correction is still urgently needed if
the revival is going to keep its balance in the
purposes of God. (*Spiritual Gifts in the Work of
the Ministry Today*)

Chapter 9 – Spiritual Gifts

Now that these ministry gifts have been described by Gee we can go on to see what he taught about spiritual gifts, understanding them as he did as mainly linked to ministries within the church. By way of introduction he laid down two principles which he felt were fundamental to a proper grasp of the subject. First of all, he maintained, the gifts of the Holy Spirit are directly related to the baptism of the Holy Spirit; it is the gateway to the gifts. This emphasis challenges the view that today's church should seek the *gifts* of the Holy Spirit but not stress a distinct *baptism* in the Holy Spirit. For Gee the two are vitally related. Secondly he maintained that spiritual gifts must be seen as distinct from natural talents, they are supernatural. The exciting contribution for Gee and his companions which the Pentecostal movement was making to the twentieth-century church was that potentially a wide spectrum of Christians could make a contribution to church life through the Holy Spirit. Class, education and culture were irrelevant. Gee was not so uncritical as to disregard natural abilities in church ministry – we remember how he spent a period each day in Edinburgh improving his own writing skills – but his point was that spiritual gifts are given as the Holy Spirit 'wills' or 'determines' and he also 'energises' or 'works' them (1 Corinthians 12: 11).

This was a two-edged sword, because Gee was also aware that Pentecostals must not try to imitate spiritual gifts; they must be real or nothing. We shall see how Gee was particularly cautious about the whole area of claims for gifts of healing. Indeed it is still an area of great perplexity within the Pentecostal movement. One of the most helpful characteristics of Gee's writing was this combination of being thoroughly Pentecostal and yet honest and realistic in his teaching.

Gee's analysis of spiritual gifts restricted them to the list found in 1 Corinthians 12: 8–10. He also felt that the order in which they were listed there by Paul implied something of their relative importance.

The first gift – *a word of wisdom* – he suggested was linked to 'apostolic government' especially in the aspect of strategy and planning. He suggests that the decision to appoint seven so-called deacons to look after the practical concerns of the Jerusalem church (Acts of the Apostles 6: 1–7) was such an exercise of the word of wisdom. The later decision of the church concerning the expansion of mission from Antioch (Acts of the Apostles 13: 2) and the council of Jerusalem's decision concerning relationships between Christians and Jews (Acts of the Apostles 15: 28) also come into this category. A weakness in Gee's comments at this point is that he fails to give what he considers to be valid modern examples of this gift in operation. But at least the standard is set for raising the level of both understanding and expectation.

The second spiritual gift was *a word of knowledge*. We have already seen how Gee parted company with most other Pentecostal teachers regarding this gift, seeing it as related to a teaching ministry.

He linked the three following gifts together as all being connected with power rather than utterance. They were the gifts of faith, healing and miracles. *Faith* is dealt with briefly by Gee. Whilst recognising that all spiritual gifts need an element of faith in their operation, he insists that the gift of faith refers to a distinct act in its own right. As an example he cites Elijah's calling down of fire and his prayer for rain. Likewise on the topic of *miracles* he simply comments

on their being great works of power such as Paul's
raising up of Eutychus who had fallen from a window
(Acts of the Apostles 20: 10).

However, on the subject of *healing* Gee was far more
expansive. He referred to it not only in *Concerning
Spiritual Gifts* and in many magazine articles, but
most notably in a further book wholly on the subject
of Pentecostal problems relating to healing, entitled
Trophimus I Left Sick. This book is again a typical
piece of Gee's writing, full of balanced biblical grasp
and wise counsel, yet not afraid to make the unpopular
observation. It is very much the mature Pentecostal
statesman writing.

Gee's teaching on healing was well within orthodox
Pentecostalism, despite the reservations and strictures
he expressed. Hence he is quite clear when he writes:

> It is absolutely hopeless to try and make any
> legitimate connections between the gifts of healing
> and medical science; or to try and claim that
> modern medical missions are the present-day
> manifestation of these spiritual gifts of the New
> Testament church. (*Concerning Spiritual Gifts*)

This did not imply that Gee discounted either medical
healing or just plain common sense in caring for
our bodies. He recognised that 'physical health is
frequently a matter of obeying simple and natural
laws of health', and that to believe in divine healing
does not exclude recourse to 'various natural means
and to the skill of the medical profession'.

However, he held the view that miracles of healing
have their 'true sphere in evangelism', rather than in
the church. Even in that sphere he suggests that gifts
of healing are not necessarily permanent – so that an
evangelist is called 'a healer' – but rather the gift is
given for the occasion. He felt that the unusual use

of the plural expression 'gifts' of healing implied such interpretation.

Believers can be anointed with oil for healing by the elders of their church (James 5:14, 15). Indeed their 'first call should be to their spiritual leaders rather than their medical advisers'; that is, they are to make a spiritual approach to the matter in the first instance and recognise that their healing may be linked to forgiveness of sins and a mutual confession of faults. Nevertheless this ministry must be distinguished from the spiritual gifts of healing. In fact Gee goes so far as to conclude:

> The church makes a profound mistake when she tries to use such spiritual gifts for herself rather than for others. (*Trophimus I Left Sick*)

Gee skilfully examines the reasons why Paul's fellow-worker, Trophimus, had to be left behind unwell and indeed unhealed. This examination he then relates to modern Pentecostal problems over healing. Any idea that Trophimus was a failure in some way must be discounted, because even Paul himself and some of his companions (such as Epaphroditus) experienced sickness. Very often it was just the 'sheer physical strain' of serving God that led to such sicknesses.

Gee goes on to develop this further by making several important observations. First, he notes that any doctrine of divine healing that professes to leave no place for pain in the present order of things is 'palpably too shallow to be true'. It did not leave any room for God's use of suffering as a means of chastisement or improvement. Then in one of Gee's best passages, he goes on to point out that ultimately we are faced with the 'problem of pain in the universe'.

> We cannot contract out of the universe as we find it, even after the supreme historical fact of

Calvary. It remains one of the final mysteries of
existence as we know it at present that God, who
is love, permits pain. (*Trophimus I Left Sick*)

Thus Gee feels that Pentecostals make many of the
problems of divine healing themselves, by 'formulating
imperfect doctrines.'

Secondly he deals with an issue at the very heart of
much Pentecostal teaching and practice about healing;
namely, whether such healing is part of the atoning
work of Christ. Actually he does not go into any great
theological analysis of this matter and others have dealt
with it more thoroughly. Nevertheless he does grasp
the nettle. Although the view that healing is in the
atonement was part of the statement of beliefs for the
British Assemblies of God and Gee was the principal
of their theological college, he still implies that he is
unhappy with the doctrine unless it is qualified.

He recognised that there were some positive aspects
to this teaching, particularly when sickness and sin
seemed closely related. Thus he comments:

The doctrine for divine healing for the body in
the atonement reaches its maximum value when
physical sickness is the result of our personal sin.
In such a case it brings unspeakable relief to the
sufferer to see that the blood of Christ purchases
not only pardon from sin, but deliverance from
its evil results in the body – 'the chastisement
of our peace was upon him and with his stripes
we are healed.' Taken very literally by multitudes
this has helped them very much and enabled
them to have faith to be healed. God be praised!
(*Trophimus I Left Sick*)

However, if this view is applied generally to all
sicknesses then it can create great practical burdens
for the sick. If they are unhealed, are they also

unsaved? Of course, all the blessings of God for
Christians lie ultimately in the cross of Christ, but
to apply this doctrine 'indiscriminately and blindly is
to plunge multitudes of good people into most grievous
problems'.

Gee concludes his discussions on this issue of healing
in the atonement by pointing out that it did not
take into account other biblical teaching such as that
found in Romans 8:16–25 and 2 Corinthians 5:1–5,
which explain that Christians are facing physical
deterioration and even death itself; indeed they await
as yet the complete 'redemption of the body'.

Overall, he notes, in this matter of healing we must
leave proper room for the will of God and not create
our own problems by going to unbiblical extremes.

The next gift of the Holy Spirit, that of *prophecy*,
is also one about which Gee makes some helpful comments, often differing significantly from the traditional
Pentecostal line. In general terms he sees prophecy as
involving a range of inspired and revelatory spoken
messages. It must be clearly distinguished from merely
preaching a sermon; and yet 'there is probably a
much larger element of prophesying in some forms of
inspirational preaching than is generally recognised.'

As we have already seen, Gee was anxious that
prophecy should not become relegated to consultations
for personal guidance in the manner of the old sooth-
sayer. His stress here is perhaps a slight over-reaction
to some sections of the Pentecostal movement where
prophecy had become trivialised. He certainly did not
rule out such biblical examples as Agabus (Acts of
the Apostles 11:28; 21:11) but felt that this kind of
prophetic ministry was of a loftier sort than everyday
enquiries. Even then Gee is prepared to go so far as as to
emphatically state: 'It can be truthfully affirmed that
there is not one single instance of the gift of prophecy
being deliberately resorted to for guidance in the New
Testament'. (*Concerning Spiritual Gifts*)

For Gee, prophecy seems to operate at various levels. There is a popular exercise, in which – in an inspirational manner – virtually all Spirit-filled Christians can praise and edify within the church gathering (Acts of the Apostles 19: 6; 1 Corinthians 14: 1). Then there is that which is linked with the ministry-gift of the prophet, where revelatory insights are given for the wider church strategy and direction (Acts of the Apostles 13: 1–3)

But perhaps Gee's most perceptive thoughts are in the linking of the spiritual gift of prophecy with aspects of the ministry-gift of the pastor, especially in an inspirational preaching role. In this context prophecy provides a 'most essential balance to the didactic and logical ministry of the teacher'. With one of his neat aphorisms, Gee observes: 'Prophecy sets on fire that which teaching enlightens.' This insight into the intermingling of gifts and ministries is one of Gee's best characteristics in his teaching on this subject. Such use of prophecy by the pastor 'can sweep the assembly up into heights of glory and enthusiasm, can melt with tenderness and make to tremble with awe. It truly ministers to the believer "edification, exhortation and comfort", and to the unbeliever can produce deep conviction. 1 Corinthians 14: 3, 24.'

In such an event, comments Gee, the ministries of pastor and teacher become mutually corrective against either intellectualism or emotionalism.

He concludes by insisting that at whatever level prophecy is found, the recipients must assess and discern the nature of the spirit of inspiration behind the authority of the prophet. It may be of the Holy Spirit, or simply the enthusiasm of the human spirit or emotion; however, sometimes it can be demonic and a lying spirit. This fact leads him to emphasise the relevance of the next spiritual gift – *the discerning of spirits*.

There are occasions when the church needs to discern

by the Holy Spirit the 'true nature of the source of any supernatural manifestation', whether it be divine or satanic. This spiritual gift, Gee notes, is about the discerning of spirits, not assessing character or motive; and such discernment is revealed supernaturally. He remarks: 'There will not only be powerful "witness" within us as to the source of the manifestation, but an actual revelation of the spirit at work.' (*Concerning Spiritual Gifts*)

This gift is only relevant in churches where the supernatural is being experienced. In a remarkable way Gee writing in 1928 was a forerunner of much that is being said today about spiritual warfare and the need to exercise such spiritual gifts as these. He felt that many were virtually unaware of the real existence of evil spirits. However, he went on:

> To the individual believer baptised in the Holy Spirit and to the assembly experiencing the operation of spiritual gifts, the whole spiritual world becomes very real. It must inevitably follow that an increasing opening of the eyes to the reality of satanic power will accompany a gracious granting of increased spiritual vision to perceive the things of God. (*Concerning Spiritual Gifts*)

Gee continued by pointing out that we should never underestimate God's provision in this gift and think that we are constantly at the mercy of Satan. Similarly this gift is not only for defence; it is also expected that recognition of evil forces will be followed by authority to banish them and to deliver those oppressed by them. He cites the incidents in Paul's ministry of Elymas and the Philippian fortune-teller as examples of this gift in action (Acts of the Apostles 13: 6–12; 16: 16–18).

Once again Gee insists on linking this gift of discernment with the ministry-gifts, especially that of the pastor protecting the flock of God. He suggests

that in most cases this spiritual gift can only be
exercised by mature and spiritual leaders whose range
of experience of the Holy Spirit's moving in church life
enables them to sense that which must be continuously
tested and if necessary resisted. At a more general level
all Christians can 'try the spirits' after the manner of 1
John 4: 1–6, but this has nothing to do with the gift of
discerning of spirits.

Finally Gee dealt with the gifts of *speaking with
tongues* and their *interpretation*. He belonged to that
early group of Pentecostal leaders who saw tongues
as an important part of Pentecostal practice and testimony. As we have already seen, he held firmly
to the view of speaking with tongues as the initial
evidence of the baptism in the Holy Spirit. In his own
public ministry, either in prayer or preaching, Gee
would interject a characteristic short phrase or two of
tongues – a sure sign that he felt under the anointing
of the Holy Spirit – and he would frequently interpret
messages given in tongues by others. This ministry
of interpretation of tongues for Gee went back to his
early years of Pentecostal experience when he recalls
how Cecil Polhill who was the leader of the Friday
evening Pentecostal meetings held in Sion College,
London, following the First World War, asked him to
'take' the interpretations from the piano where Gee
was accompanying the singing.

Speaking with tongues is seen by Gee as a most
helpful provision through the Holy Spirit for allowing
true spiritual emotion to be expressed. He suggests that
it was 'quite a logical outcome from an intense fullness
of emotion'. It was a 'spontaneous expression of otherwise unutterable ecstasy', and 'the understanding was
temporarily suspended under the rush of spiritual
feeling'. Gee held to the interesting idea that just
as human speech, or the tongue (James 3: 6), was
somehow central to the whole personality either for
good or evil, for that reason speaking with tongues

represented 'the flag of the victor ... upon the most significant part of the captured soul'. He also felt that it was the 'abasement of all pride of intellect'.

Gee was one of the few early Pentecostal leaders to try to understand the nature of speaking in tongues, rather than just its significance or practice. He anticipated some of the more recent psychological studies of the phenomenon. He wrote:

> Comparatively few have understood the real nature of the divine inspiration behind the tongues. For many people it has been a supposedly mechanical operation of the Spirit of God by which he has spoken through their human vocal organs while their own personality has been dormant. (*Concerning Spiritual Gifts*)

Gee sought to show that it is 'quite un-scriptural to say that the Holy Spirit speaks in tongues'. The inspiration is of the Holy Spirit and fully supernatural, but the mechanics are of the human spirit; he quotes with approval: 'If I pray in a tongue, my spirit prays, but my mind is unfruitful' (1 Corinthians 14: 14), And he notes humorously that when Pentecostals speak with tongues, it is not 'members of the Blessed Trinity holding converse with each other through some human channel!'

He concluded on this understanding of the nature of speaking with tongues:

> The surge of divine emotion that produced the manifestation was genuinely supernatural; it was the fulness of the Spirit of God within man: but under that inspiring power it was the human spirit that prayed, and sang and gave thanks in a tongue. To hold a right theory of inspiration is absolutely essential to a right understanding of spiritual gifts. (*Concerning Spiritual Gifts*)

As with his teaching about other gifts of the Holy Spirit,
so Gee sought to relate the public use of tongues to
various ministry-gifts within the church. Like many
others he considered tongues accompanied by interpretation to be equivalent to prophecy, although he
felt they should have a more devotional element to
them than prophecy. He also suggested that tongues
and interpretation were used too frequently in many
assemblies, mistakenly because some thought that was
the only true mark of the supernatural in a meeting.
Gee's view was that such manifestations should com-
plement and enhance other ministries, such as teaching
or inspirational prophetic preaching, that were taking
place at the time. One can see that Gee was shrewdly
protesting against a pattern of Pentecostal meetings
where tongues and interpretation were restricted to
the times of open prayer and frequently performed in a
perfunctory and repetitive manner. Gee's dictum seems
to have been: fewer tongues, but more significant.

Perceptions of this kind about the nature of spiritual
gifts led Gee on in his writings to deal with a range
of practical and pastoral issues in the general area
of conduct and holiness, many of which were linked
to ministries and spiritual gifts. It is to this second
main aspect of his teaching ministry that we must
now turn.

Chapter 10 – Fruits of the Spirit

Gee completed his expositions of major Pentecostal themes – gifts and ministries – with a third series on the fruit of the Spirit. He used the former themes regularly in his early international ministry, and the idea of completing the series with a study of the fruit of the Spirit was suggested to him by the Filadelfia Pentecostal Church in Stockholm when they invited him to return for a second visit to their annual Bible school in 1931. During a voyage to South Africa in 1934 Gee wrote up the studies for publication under the title *The Fruit of the Spirit*. Many years later in 1961 he again expanded the series into a new volume entitled *Fruitful or Barren?*. He acknowledged that much had already been said and written about these characteristics of Christian living enumerated in Galatians 5: 22, 23, but he wanted to approach them 'from a distinctly Pentecostal standpoint'. Moreover, he intended particularly to apply the series to those engaged in Pentecostal ministry. Hence, as we shall see, Gee was once more anchoring his teaching in the familiar areas of gifts and ministries, rather than Christian life in general.

Despite the strong Pentecostal emphasis Gee was at pains to point out that the fruit of the Spirit did not originate from the baptism in the Spirit but rather from the regenerating and sanctifying work of the Spirit of Christ at work in all Christians. He stressed this for two reasons:

It shows how it is possible for believers who

have received the Spirit in regenerating power as the Spirit of Christ who dwells with them, to manifest much of His 'fruit' without their ever receiving a definite experience of the baptism in the Holy Spirit. And on the other hand, it reveals how possible it is for believers to exercise certain gifts of the Spirit received through the Baptism, without showing forth the fruit of the Spirit. (*The Fruit of the Spirit*)

Once this point about the source of the fruit of the Spirit had been clarified, Gee quickly moved on to what was his main objective; to show the important relationship and value that this fruit has to the exercise of Pentecostal gifts and ministries. The gifts and ministries should never be an end in themselves, and need to be constantly complemented by the fruits of Christ-like personality and behaviour. Only then would such manifestations of the Holy Spirit build up or expand the church. The correct approach and balance is found in Paul's injunction: 'Follow after love and desire spiritual gifts' (1 Corinthians 14:1).

In a passage so relevant and contemporary to some current situations, Gee remarks on the devastation caused when Pentecostal ministries and the fruit of the Spirit are not matched. He writes:

The gifted evangelist often can conceal moral failure for a time, in the glow of great crowds attracted by healings, but ultimately the moral weakness will come out. Then the bitter disappointment of the people can easily lead new converts to throw away their faith in the gospel. They need not, and often will not, throw away their faith in Christ if they have come so far, but we must face the facts that for new converts it is the personality of the evangelist that counts most. It is all very well

to say that we must 'look beyond the man to
God', but that is asking a lot for the spiritually
immature. Their tiny faith in God has received a
cruel blow almost before it has been born, if the
one who has been to them in the place of God turns
out a disappointment. (*Fruitful or Barren?*)

Following on from this he draws out a similar application for the use of spiritual gifts in assembly life. With
characteristic frankness and perception he comments:

The speaker in tongues who lacks love is like 'a
noisy gong or a clanging cymbal' (Moffat): that
is to say he is merely a headache! A true gift
of tongues exercised by a believer radiant with
the love of God is a manifestation of exquisite
beauty and rarely repels any normal person. But
the true spring of the beauty is in the character of
the speaker and not in the fluency of the gift. We
are slow to learn that true spiritual power is in
Pentecostal *personalities* [Gee's italics], by which
is meant men and women filled with and sanctified
by the Spirit of God rather than in spiritual
gifts themselves. We are even more reluctant
to acknowledge that a display of Pentecostal
gifts without corresponding holiness can be so
barren of results as to profit nothing. (*Fruitful
or Barren?*)

These teachings by Gee are all in keeping with his valuable insight into the whole inter-relationship between
gifts, ministries and fruit which seem so frequently to
be overlooked in practice. If Gee made one great contribution to a biblical understanding of the Pentecostal
experience then surely it is in this area. The thrust of
what Gee wants us to know is that these attributes of
being a Pentecostal Christian must never be isolated,

but always seen and practised as a whole. It is only then, he feels, that the maximum manifestation of spiritual power and achievement for God will be realised.

Much that Gee says about the ninefold fruit of the Spirit is a repetition of what can be found in any good devotional commentary on the subject. However here I want us to note some of the specific Pentecostal applications which he seeks to draw out as well. Along with most other teachers he identifies *love* as a comprehensive description for all the fruit of the Spirit. The other eight – joy, peace, patience, kindness, goodness, faithfulness, gentleness and self-control – are characteristics of the one true fruit of love. Gee sees love as having an overall application in Pentecostal ministry, in that it enables various charismatic gifts and ministries to be used in unattractive and arduous situations. Gifts on their own, observes Gee, are quite useless if the power of love for loveless people is not there to motivate such gifts into action. He notes:

Love for the unlovely becomes a reality, and also a necessity, for missionaries, pastors, social workers ... God's shepherds need the fruit of the Spirit every bit as much as the gifts of the Spirit – perhaps more? (*Fruitful or Barren?*)

Perceptively, Gee goes on to point out that love is costly and the exercise of a supernatural ministry frequently brings opposition and misunderstanding. It is these situations which demand the self-sacrifice of love which when combined with gifts and ministries produces an effective work. In contrast to this Gee reflects that it costs little to exercise spiritual gifts in 'sympathetic circles'; on the contrary it can become obsessive for some and can lead to a kind of monopoly of use and even spiritual pride. One wonders what Gee would have made of some of the cosy conferences in salubrious retreat centres today, with the somewhat introverted use of gifts within the groups themselves.

So, for Gee, love is the ingredient *par excellence*, which must be combined with spiritual gifts to make them edifying and of lasting value. He is surely right in his insistence that in Paul's teaching about spiritual gifts and love in 1 Corinthians 12–14, they are not being contrasted as alternatives but *combined* as essential complements to each other in a truly Pentecostal ministry within the church and the world.

The fruit of *joy*, insists Gee, must be seen as something deep within the experience and not seen as on the surface. From a Pentecostal standpoint, he is anxious to distinguish between the true emotion of joy in the Holy Spirit as against mere excitement and sensation created by a superficial use of spiritual gifts. These true depths are often felt and expressed through the gifts of tongues. Moreover, Gee's keen insight here is that we do not speak in tongues to create joy or feelings; rather we should be so engaged in Christ's service, or worshipping in his presence, that the deep joy felt within us can only be expressed with the 'joy unspeakable and full of glory' which tongues allows. To put it the other way round is, says Gee, 'one of the cruellest mistakes we can ever make in the Spirit-filled life', for it leads to the externalising of joy in the form of seeking continual manifestations. The mistake then 'becomes deadly if manifestations become, first forced, and then finally imitated by the flesh'. Gee's view is both liberating and energising. It liberates us from creating a pretence of joy on the surface, as if it were the only valid hallmark of our Pentecostalism, but it also motivates us to ongoing service when the Holy Spirit creates those deep feelings of joy within us confirming our ministry in Christ despite the persecution and frustration often experienced. Indeed it was Jesus himself who 'for the joy set before him' endured the cross (Hebrews 12: 2).

While recognising the wider understanding of the fruit of *peace* as inward calm, Gee also suggests that within the use of Pentecostal gifts and ministries the fruit of peace should be created in individuals and assemblies. No effective leadership ministry-gift of Christ should produce division or rivalry, as sadly happened in Corinth with the successors to Paul and Apollos. Similarly the exercise of spiritual gifts in the assembly should not create confusion or disorder. Here Gee has in mind the uncontrolled use of prophecy and tongues. These gifts in particular, says Gee, must be used in conjunction with the fruit of peace in order to be most effective and edifying: 'For God is not a God of disorder but of peace' (1 Corinthians 14: 33). It would seem that Paul's injunction that the spirits of the prophets should be 'subject to the control of the prophets' (1 Corinthians 14: 31), meant in effect that the gift of prophecy must be complemented by the fruit of peace in order to be in the Spirit and beneficial to the life of the church. Gee felt this to be particularly the case where an element of 'rebuking' comes into prophecies. He concludes: 'All too often it is the manifestation of a soured and frustrated human spirit not right with God.' However, where spiritual gifts and ministries create peace then it becomes one of the church's 'greatest assets, for it clears the road for unhampered evangelism and fruitful growth in grace among the converts'.

The fruit of *patience* and *kindness* which Gee advocates are essential accompaniments for gifts of leadership, especially the ministry-gift of the pastor. He also included the ministry of 'governments' or 'administration' (1 Corinthians 12: 28) in this category. Patience and kindness in dealing with individuals or piloting the vessel of the church are essential fruit to underlie gifts of leadership. He contrasted such leadership with

the more dramatic and provocative ministries of the
evangelist and prophet. In this context Gee was fond
of quoting Paul: 'Even though you have ten thousand
guardians in Christ, you do not have many fathers' (1
Corinthians 4: 15).

It was a constant emphasis in Gee's teaching that
holiness of life must undergird any use of spiritual
gifts or ministry-gifts. They are, after all, the gifts of
the Holy Spirit and must reflect his nature if they
are to be effective in the church. It is in this sense
of personal holiness that Gee particularly understood
the significance of the fruit of *goodness* in relation to
Pentecostal life. In his writings about it he frequently
adopts the role of the Pentecostal apologist. Many
have criticised evangelists and others who demonstrate
gifts of the Spirit but later on are found to have
moral failings, especially relating to money and sex.
Gee sought to explain this by pointing out that in
biblical examples in both the Old Testament and
the New Testament the 'manifestations of the Spirit
are not in exact ratio to the degree of holiness'.
Rather God's grace and man's faith frequently play
a part in these apparent contradictions. Moreover,
the Lord 'does not wait for near-perfection in those
he deigns to use'. In fact, says Gee, to manifest
spiritual gifts is not particularly a sign of holiness
anyway.

He used to like telling the story of an American
camp meeting he had attended in the early 1930s.
Fish had been served for breakfast. Later on, as Gee
was speaking, he drank some water and it tasted
fishy! He commented, 'The water was pure and fresh
but it was spoiled by the flavour imparted by the
vessel.'

This led Gee to his conclusions on goodness and
holiness in relation to spiritual gifts and ministries.
Without the fruit of goodness the maximum effective-
ness of such gifts will be undermined and diminished.

Thus anyone who begins to know the blessings of exercising such gifts must strive towards holiness of character in order to be glorifying to God and edifying to the church. Although our prayer for gifted people is often 'Give them more power, Lord', perhaps it should be: 'Give them more purity' – the fruit of goodness.

The fruit of *faithfulness* needs to be distinguished from the spiritual gift of faith. It is, says Gee, loyalty or reliability, reflecting the very faithfulness and covenant loyalty of God himself. He quotes with approval the illustration often used by Howard Carter, of the somewhat shiftless human personality being like dry or loose cement; when the living water of the Holy Spirit is poured into it, a solid and reliable texture emerges. This is the fruit of steadfastness. Gee particularly attaches the significance of this fruit to ministry-gifts in general, in terms of being faithful to our gifting or calling. Hardship, apathy or the temptation to use our gifts in a more lucrative career all need to be resisted by the fruit of faithfulness.

Finally the fruits of *meekness* and *self-control* are described. Gee suggests that meekness is similar to self-control and the earlier-mentioned fruit of patience and gentleness. However, the key difference is that meekness is more an inward attitude of spirit, and the very opposite of the spirit of this world. It is the inward characteristic of strength under control which then gives rise to the outward acts of patience, gentleness and self-control. Such a fruit of meekness means that there is no inner build-up of resentment or frustration because we are having to be patient with others. Gee comments:

> Gentleness can sometimes be used when the spirit does not feel gentle, but if the heart is not really meek the inward fire of anger and pride will

inevitably reveal itself sooner or later. (*The Fruit
of the Spirit*)

One of the constant emphases of Gee's teaching in
the churches concerned the repetitive use of certain
spiritual gifts in public gatherings. He felt that self-
control over one's spirit and emotions meant that the
disorderly use of speaking with gifts of the Spirit
could be avoided. In this context he would quote
1 Corinthians 14: 18–19, 26–28, 32, as the biblical
pattern. I well remember hearing him preach on a text
which I gather he frequently used in some of the more
'unruly' assemblies: 'If you find honey, eat just enough
– too much of it and you will vomit' (Proverbs 25: 16).
He then went on, in that gruff yet winsome way, to
point out that 'two or at most three spoonsful of honey'
were enough messages in tongues for a Pentecostal
meeting!

In one of his lesser-known books *This is the Will
of God – The Bible and Sexual Problems* (1940) Gee
gave a helpful insight into one area of self-control
in which he sought again to combine down-to-earth
insights with Pentecostal theology and experience. If
the more emotional gifts of worship are used outside
the controlled purposes of ministry, they can lead to
sexual immorality within such introspective groups or
occasions. Gee suggests that there is a narrow margin
between spirit, soul and body:

Let the emotions gain control in defiance of the
Holy Spirit of grace; let the personality become
subject to mere pleasure in an unrestrained orgy
of sheer feeling, even though it be originally religious feeling; and before long the baser physical
passions will assert themselves. (*This is the Will
of God*)

That this whole subject of sexuality was a concern for

the Pentecostal churches is shown by Gee's opening
remarks:

> Some few years ago while attending a large con-
> ference of Pentecostal ministers, I was approached
> with the suggestion that I might write a frank
> book on the question of the sex life from the
> standpoint of those who know the fulness of the
> Holy Spirit.

What is also interesting is that although we are more
familiar with such books in Christian circles today, Gee
was again ahead of his time by writing as he did at the
end of the 1930s. It is an eminently practical book,
and despite the reserved nature of its author shows
him again as being a first-rate pastoral teacher and
communicator.

In concluding our description of Gee's teaching
on the fruit of the Holy Spirit we note the way
he insisted on combining their proper understanding
with spiritual gifts and ministry gifts; in this he
reveals a balanced and true definition of holiness.
Holiness in its basic meaning implies 'separation',
but it is separation unto service and the good of
others that makes it true fruit of the Holy Spirit. For
this emphasis within Pentecostalism we are much
indebted to Donald Gee.

During the 1930s and 1940s a steady flow of pastoral
books came from Gee's pen. Most were collections
of materials on practical issues which he regularly
preached and taught during his international travels.
Some had marvellous titles such as *Keeping in Touch*
and *Laughter and Tears*; others were more straightforward as with *Studies in Guidance* and *Proverbs for
Pentecost*.

One book which was first published at the beginning
of this period in 1930 and frequently reprinted, eventually being revised in 1952, was *Concerning Shepherds*

and Sheepfolds – a series of studies dealing with
pastors and assemblies. It was a typically clear and
valuable guide for Pentecostal pastors, struggling as
Gee had done in Edinburgh, with the leadership of a
small, pioneer church and often with no theological
college training or experience.

Gee deals wisely and perceptively with issues such
as a pastor's calling and character. Some of the topics
reveal the particular debates going on within the new
freedoms of the Pentecostal assemblies – should they
have official membership roles; and is it right to form
separate Pentecostal assemblies, separating from the
main church denominations?

Although in his later years Gee was to be among
the first to welcome the renewal movement within
the historic denominations, in those early years of
strident opposition to Pentecostalism he saw the need
for separation.

> There are times when division is a sign of life and
> union a sign of deterioration and death . . . The
> Pentecostal experience sooner or later demands
> the Pentecostal assembly. When believers have
> received the gifts of the Holy Spirit according
> to 1 Corinthians 12: 8–11, it is impossible, and
> downright wrong, for them to bury themselves
> in congregations where experience of such gifts
> is neither allowed nor accepted. (*Shepherds and
> Sheepfolds*)

Other topics included the financial support of the
pastor; church discipline; how to conduct the church
services, with both freedom and control; and lastly how
to train new workers. All of these were areas where
Gee stamped his image on a growing range of young
Pentecostal churches and ministers throughout the
world. His contribution to the stabilising of these early,
often erratic, assemblies – a contribution made mainly

through his writings – must not be underestimated. And of course they were read in those somewhat narrow days not because other books on pastoral theology were not available, but because they were written by an experienced Pentecostal teacher for fellow Pentecostal believers.

III. MATURE LEADERSHIP

Chapter 11 – Pentecostal Historian

Although the 1940s were to be somewhat flat years in the Pentecostal movement because of the restrictions on travel and economic crises which followed World War II, nevertheless they were important years in the life of Donald Gee. We have already seen how during the 1930s he had established himself as an international teacher of repute and gained a remarkable personal insight into Pentecostalism worldwide. The following decade was to see him become an international Pentecostal statesman, for two main reasons: his writing of the first major history of Pentecostalism, and then his appointment as the first editor of the official magazine of the World Pentecostal Fellowship.

Gee was no formal historian; but he had two strengths which enabled him to produce his *magnum opus* on the history of Pentecostalism. One was that he had met with a remarkably wide range of Pentecostal leaders, often visiting their countries and churches and frequently staying in their homes. As a result of this he possessed a personal knowledge of the origins and development of the Pentecostal movement unparalleled among his peers and frequently updated by regular correspondence. Secondly Gee had an orderly mind which had already been put to good use in his systematic teaching ministry. Now, coupled with his narrative and lucid writing skills, these resources were to combine in the publishing of a Pentecostal history.

The first edition of *The Pentecostal Movement* appeared in 1941 and was updated in 1949. Towards the end of his life, Gee worked steadily on a revision and enlargement of this history, sometimes lamenting, 'I shall be dead before the book is published'! In fact he did manage to complete it, but the new edition entitled *Wind and Flame* was published in 1967 shortly after his death in the previous year.

In the introduction to the 1941 edition Gee sets out his reasons for writing:

> The generation who participated in the rise of what has come to be called the Pentecostal Movement is swiftly passing away. We owe it to our children to place in their hands, as true a record as may be of the beginning of the Movement with which their parents, either natural or spiritual, have been identified, and with whose progress many of them are still deeply concerned. (*Wind and Flame*)

However, Gee was perceptive enough to recognise that a revival movement and history are to some extent self-contradictory, or at least unhappy bedfellows. While on the one hand a history shows that the revival was not short-lived or superficial, on the other hand it can imply to many that the movement has become institutionalised. Of the latter Gee comments:

> To them it sounds ominous. The morning is passed. Whence is the movement now trending? The pioneers of 'Pentecost' visualised a revival that was to touch and inspire every section of the Christian church; for they belonged to so many different sections. Above all things, their hearts glowed with the expectation and conviction that this was destined to be the last revival before

the coming of the Lord, and that for them, all earthly history would soon be consummated by the 'Rapture'. (*Wind and Flame*)

Gee's response to this widely-prevailing attitude was of the kind which puts him into the category of an international Pentecostal statesman. He was beginning to educate his fellow Pentecostalists and gently urge them to recognise that their movement must be seen as part of the wider history of the Christian church. Similarly they must not remain in the revivalist stage for ever, but begin to anticipate consolidation and organisation as part of God's plan for making their movement one of ongoing fruitfulness.

Hence Gee continued:

That hope (the return of Christ) remains: but the passing decades, the inevitable development produced by the formation of distinctive Pentecostal assemblies, the resultant rise of organisation, and finally recognised denominationalism, has now produced a situation and an outlook vastly different from that which pertained at the beginning. The clock cannot be put back. But the vision can still inspire and direct. The significance of the movement should be interpreted. (*Wind and Flame*)

So Gee's history was the first co-ordinated act of self-interpretation within the worldwide Pentecostal movement. It would be wrong to read it as purely objective history; it was written with prophetic insight by a man seeking to encourage his fellow Pentecostalists to engage in a process of self-assessment and self-interpretation that would take them forward in the post-war era as a significant force within the whole spectrum of Christianity. In this sense Gee, back in the

1940s, was already anticipating the neo-Pentecostal revival of the 1960s which he was to welcome and which led to Pentecostalism being described as the 'third force in Christianity' alongside Protestantism and Roman Catholicism. Although this has yet to be substantially researched, Gee's history also provided a historical introduction and background for the emerging neo-charismatic movement from which it could gain its own sense of history and direction. Thus his historical work was very much a statesmanlike bridging of the old and the new – a revival beginning to see itself as a movement, and classical Pentecostalism beginning to widen into an ecumenical charismatic renewal of church life and experience.

One final general observation on Gee's history of Pentecostalism is to note its apologetic value and contribution. Even in the early 1940s the movement was still widely shunned and criticised. However Gee's book gave an opportunity for church leaders to read for themselves a comprehensive and reasonably objective account. As Gilbert Kirby wrote in the foreword of the final edition:

> The account of the Pentecostal Movement he gives is fair, honest and up-to-date. No man knew the Movement more intimately than he. As one would have expected, his appraisal is balanced and sincere. He does not attempt to cover up some of the problems within their own ranks with which the Pentecostalists have had to contend ... The whole book is marked by an eirenical spirit and shows how over the years Pentecostalists have gained increasing acceptance in the eyes of their fellow Christians.

The main aim of Gee's history was to give a chronological survey of the Pentecostal movement. In the earlier part of his book he devotes whole chapters to single important and formative years and events, such as the Azusa Street revival in Los Angeles during 1906, generally regarded as the beginning of modern Pentecostalism. Gee possessed one of the few photographs of the original wooden mission church building, taken personally during his first visit in the late 1920s shortly before the building was demolished. This photograph was included in the earlier editions.

Similarly, he devotes a complete chapter to the year 1907 and the beginnings of Pentecostalism in Britain under the leadership of Alexander Boddy in Sunderland, following the visit of Thomas B. Barrett, the Pentecostal Methodist leader from Oslo. When subsequently Gee met Barrett on several occasions and stayed in his home in Norway such meetings must have been opportunities to glean many personal details of the early history of Pentecostalism.

After dealing with the earlier formative years, Gee began to widen the scope of his material, dealing with periods of about five years at a time, so taking the story of the movement forward through to the beginnings of the neo-Pentecostal revival in the 1960s. He skilfully traces the beginnings of the Pentecostal movement in many countries and then returns to them in later chapters with further descriptions of their progress and development. Such progress was particularly related to the great evangelistic healing crusades of Smith Wigglesworth and the Jeffreys brothers in the 1930s, and then of Oral Roberts and T.L. Osborn in the 1950s, along with several others described by Gee. He also sensitively emphasises occasions when Pentecostalism was beginning to feel its own identity as a movement, particularly through international conferences. Hence the European conferences in Amsterdam in 1921 and Stockholm in 1939 are ably described by Gee, who was both a participant at the first and an organiser of the second. But it is to the world conferences – first in Zurich in 1947, when the World Pentecostal

Conference was formed under the secretaryship of
David du Plessis, and then afterwards in Paris in 1949
and London in 1952 – that Gee gives special attention
and description. He saw these conferences as extremely
important occasions in self-awareness; for him they
were the Pentecostal movement's coming-of-age.

His history ends with a sympathetic account of
the charismatic renewal occurring within the historic
denominations to create what he aptly described as
a 'double river of blessing'. The story, which for Gee
coincided so much with his own life and involvement,
was one of the small beginnings of the Pentecostal
movement, now becoming an international movement
of repute and recognised as the fastest growing movement within Christianity.

Gee's account of the history of the Pentecostal
movement has its strengths and weaknesses. His
work was not that of a critical historian and so
cannot be measured against the vast scope and detail
of the historical writings of such scholars as Walter
Hollenweger. Similarly there is not the consistency
of treatment one looks for in a professional history; if
anything Gee's work is patchy in places and gives too
much description of the British situation as against the
world-wide development. Moreover Gee did not have
the benefit of the remarkable growth of Pentecostal
research which has taken place in many universities
today and so his sources were obviously limited and
often subjective. If anything he was more of a journalist
than a historian. Nevertheless his history is of great
value for the reasons already set out at the beginning
of this chapter. It is also a warm and readable account.
Much of the strength lies in the vast number of
Pentecostal leaders Gee had met in his travels, coupled
with the fact that he was a perceptive observer and
recorder of events and personalities. In this sense,
Gee's writings are as much source materials as mere
co-ordinated history.

This enabled him to give greater detail and insight into the development of some aspects of Pentecostalism. For example he visited Douglas Scott, the pioneer of Pentecostalism in France, on several occasions during the 1930s; and so he provides one of the few personal glimpses of this remarkable ministry, describing some of the healings and conversions which led to church growth in France. He relates Scott's account of the conversion of a theatre clown:

> He used to make others laugh on the stage, but went behind the scenes to cry because of his misery and sickness. One day on coming back from a tour, he was surprised to meet a little girl, who had been a cripple and walked with crutches, trotting gaily downstairs. This completely staggered him and that very night he was at our meetings where the Lord saved and healed him. He immediately gave up his job on stage and the Lord found him other work, so that after his baptism in the Holy Spirit he placed his gifts on the altar for the Lord and today is the ex-clown who conducts the singing in the assembly. (*Wind and Flame*)

From this personal involvement Gee was able to sum up the account of the development of Pentecostalism in France with the following assessment:

> The planting of the Assemblies of God in France was marked by wise planning and leadership. Useful conferences of the French ministers were held at frequent intervals, when more experienced brethren, often from England, would take counsel with them and open up the Scriptures. Thus the work was saved from many pitfalls through experience. (*Wind and Flame*)

In the same way Gee's close association and numerous

visits to the Filadelfia church in Stockholm under the
leadership of Lewi Pethrus gave him the opportunity to describe to a wide audience the depth of the
growth which had taken place in Sweden in the 1920s
and 30s.

Having described the pastoral team, Gee adds first-
hand detail of the wider situation in the Filadelphia
church at the end of the 1930s:

> In addition to all these leading preachers, there
> are about forty elders and deacons who take
> an active and valuable part in assisting in the
> care of this great flock of the Lord's people.
> [In 1938 the membership was given by Gee as
> totalling 5,887.] As for the manifold activities of
> this powerful assembly, there is a Sunday School
> for children, which with thirty branch schools,
> has a total of 1,800 scholars and 214 teachers.
> There is an inspiring philanthropic work, where
> 400 to 500 unemployed or needy men are regularly
> given free meals; and fifty-two homeless men get
> a bed for ten consecutive nights in a large barge
> moored near the assembly, comfortably fitted and
> well-named with delightful wit – 'The Ark'. (*Wind
> and Flame*)

A final comment about Gee's historical writing which
illustrates its value is that he gave a number of his
own evaluations or interpretive summaries at the end
of major sections in his book. These comments were
meant to be instructive to his fellow Pentecostals
and to be a guide for their own understanding and
practices during the post-World War II era, as well
as an apologetic for the wider reader.

For example, after describing the early stages of
the Pentecostal movement, Gee pauses to comment
on the fierce opposition it roused and why that should

have been the case. He suggests that some criticisms came from genuine misunderstanding and the excesses which sometimes happened in the young Pentecostal churches. However he perceptively points out that 'very few notable personalities' whose reputation and influence could have prevented misunderstanding, were connected with the new movement. Yet his most thoughtful observation came in his concluding comment:

> Finally, there seems to be a law which students are compelled to observe, that the last wave of spiritual revival in the church nearly always seems to offer the greatest opposition to the new wave of oncoming blessing and advance. It must be remembered, and that with deep sympathy, that when the teaching and testimony of the Pentecostal Movement came to the front there were great numbers of Christian leaders who already were claiming to have been baptised in the Holy Spirit in connection with preceding revival movements. Only a most gracious spirit and an unusual humility of mind, could accept the new and more scriptural standards which, certainly not always wisely nor winsomely, the Pentecostal preachers now set up. Where that challenge to seek, receive and manifest at least something of apostolic Christian experience in the Spirit was not accepted, the obvious line of excuse and self-defence was to repudiate and finally slander, the Movement that provoked it. Delicate though the point may be, we are compelled to recognise that here we touch a fundamental reason for much of the opposition. (*Wind and Flame*)

This kind of writing is characteristic of many of Gee's contributions; on the one hand gently rebuking those with a tendency to immaturity in the Pentecostal

movement and on the other hand firmly refusing to
compromise the testimony of the Pentecostal experience at its most biblical.

Some years later, when Pentecostal denominations
had begun to be organised and Gee had been describing
the groups in Britain who taught that the office of
apostle and prophet should be reinstated within the
local church, he concluded:

> With this ideal one can have much sympathy.
> But one great cause of failure has always been
> the lack of distinguishing between mere *names*
> [Gee's italics] of scriptural offices and the *fact*
> of the office in reality and power. To bestow
> New Testament titles of offices upon men and
> women and then consider that by so doing we
> are creating apostolic assemblies parallel to those
> of the primitive church, is very much like children
> playing at churches. It is the plain fact of the real
> spiritual gift and ministry within the individual
> that makes any office, and then the mere title is
> a secondary matter. As a matter of fact the gifts
> and offices set by God through the Holy Spirit
> in the church often exist where their scriptural
> designations are never thought of. (*Wind and
> Flame*)

The 1930s were an era of growth and expansion for
Pentecostalism, especially by means of large evangelistic healing campaigns. Gee spends some time
describing that exciting period of Pentecostal history,
but then completes his account with an overall assessment of such campaigns in relation to the Pentecostal
movement as a whole. He pointed out that such 'signs
and wonders' evangelism was quite biblical and that,
though much of the ministry was quite new to the evangelists and there were few precedents to guide them,
'they gained experience as they went on', especially

in the area of media publicity; claims regarding the numbers involved were sometimes over-ambitious.

However Gee had certain general observations to make which, one feels, have an abiding significance. First of all he pointed out:

> Campaign characteristics tend to linger in result-ant assemblies and this factor, more than any other, has left a permanent impress on the out-ward form of the Movement. At first certain methods may seem almost necessary to retain the crowds, but permanent lightness, or emphasis on the spectacular for its own sake, begets spir-itual pauperism. The singing of many choruses provided a dominant feature of big campaigns, and now remains as a permanent item. Some of the choruses are beautiful and helpful, but others of the 'jazz' type would be better buried without delay. Above all else, the flock of God cries out to be *fed* [Gee's italics]. Assembly life is not one constant 'campaign' in the accepted sense of the word, though it *is* a constant manifestation of the love of God in Christ seeking the lost. (*Wind and Flame*)

Secondly he made some shrewd comments about the effect of such campaigns on the true nature of the Pentecostal experience. He wrote:

> The great campaigns tended to shift the emphasis of the Pentecostal testimony from the baptism in the Holy Spirit over to divine healing. Some of the new assemblies that resulted were scarcely recog-nisable for a time as truly 'Pentecostal' at all.

He continued:

> Baptisms in the Spirit tended to become lighter.

> There were not the prolonged tarrying meetings
> and corresponding self-emptying, with such ulti-
> mate depth of blessing to their whole subsequent
> experience. (*Wind and Flame*)

However Gee sought to give an objective assessment
when he concluded:

> Our judgement needs guarding against the intoxi-
> cation of huge crowds and scenes of deep enthusi-
> asm. The passing success of a visiting evangelist
> in a locality ought never to be compared with those
> profound spiritual movements that have changed
> the course of history. On the other hand it is
> foolish to refuse to acknowledge the large amount
> of good work truly accomplished. The permanent
> results of the great campaigns have been impres-
> sive enough, even when every discount has been
> allowed. For these it ought to be our delight to
> glorify God. (*Wind and Flame*)

Gee's flowing style, his colourful personal anecdotes
and reminiscences, and the overall interest and stirring
nature of the content make this history hard to put
down. Yet it is the intermittent comment and interpretive observation as the story unfolds which raise
Gee's book above mere excitement or nostalgia and
reveals the statesmanlike contribution which he made
to the Pentecostal movement through this valuable
historical work.

Chapter 12 – Pentecostal Statesman

In 1947 an opportunity came to Gee that was to elevate him to an even greater international role and status within the Pentecostal movement: he was invited to become the first editor of a worldwide magazine to be known as *Pentecost*. The first World Pentecostal Conference held in Zurich in 1947 had discussed the initiating of a quarterly magazine that would concentrate mainly on what was termed 'worldwide Pentecostal missionary and revival news'. Lewi Pethrus, the Scandinavian leader, had proposed Donald Gee as the editor commenting:

> He knows the Pentecostal Movement all over the world better than most of us and he is a man with vision and a deep spiritual knowledge of the Pentecostal Movement.

There were to be no editorial restrictions on Gee, which was an indication of respect the Conference had for his objectivity. Gee commented on this in his first editorial noting:

> The editor will endeavour, according to the grace given unto him, to keep loyal to his trust and avoid any partiality. Our intention is to seek the glory of God alone by reviewing Pentecostal activity irrespective of any denominational or ideological connection. (*Pentecost*, September 1947)

This appointment was but the conclusion and outward result of a much deeper concern shared by Gee and many other leaders in the 1940s, that Pentecostalism should have a greater worldwide unity. His travels had given him much broader perspectives on the international Pentecostal movement than the more parochial and localised views held by some of his fellow leaders. Gee could see the need for discussions, information and co-operation at a worldwide level. He had been part of the organisation committee for the first World Pentecostal Conference in Zurich in 1947, where these visions were first openly discussed. Three years later in Paris he was part of the leadership group which recommended that the World Conference should be held every three years, forming a loose-knit world Pentecostal organisation. It was in Zurich and Paris that the friendship and alliance between Gee and David du Plessis began to emerge around these common objectives. Du Plessis, though secretary of the World Pentecostal Conference organisation for a few years, was soon to follow a more independent line of dialogue with the historic churches. Nevertheless he and Gee shared a similar vision and their friendship remained constant.

Gee was in no way trying to encourage the formation of a worldwide Pentecostal denomination, but he was part of a group who saw that the Pentecostal movement should have an awareness of a worldwide self-identity. To those who felt that such organisations led to static institutionalism, Gee responded with characteristic fire:

It is individuals who backslide – not movements. It is individuals who retain the anointing – not movements. It is new MEN [Gee's capitals] whom God will raise up and bless – not new movements . . . Membership of the true Pentecostal Movement is not membership of any sect, or denomination, or organisation, or even any local Pentecostal church. True membership of such a movement is being filled with the Holy Spirit 'as at the beginning' and continuing in that fullness. (*Wind and Flame*)

Gee felt that true Pentecostal unity was the New Testament pattern of unity in the Spirit. In an editorial shortly after the Paris conference entitled 'Possible Pentecostal Unity' he skilfully seeks to show how he understands such unity for the international Pentecostal movement. With the insight that set him apart as a world leader he wrote:

How much of that scriptural Pentecostal unity can we enjoy today? The World Pentecostal Conferences in Zurich and Paris made it plain that the kind of unity embodied in one world-wide Pentecostal denomination is impossible. It is equally impossible to unite over a particular ideology that would help all who participate eschew forms of organisation they deem legitimate and helpful. Further discussion on the point is futile. The only possible unity lies in cultivating pentecostal principles upon which all have always been agreed. The purpose, as we understand it, of resolving to hold regular World Pentecostal Conferences, and of appointing a Secretary with an Advisory Committee to arrange the same, is to provide a means of promoting and keeping a possible Pentecostal unity of tremendous potentiality for untold good. We can be enriched by sharing the things God has taught us by revelation and by experience in doctrine and practice. We can explore many possibilities of practical co-operation in evangelism, whether by missionary work, broadcasting or literature. We can investigate common problems.

Mischievous misunderstandings can be cleared away by speaking face to face. The mere fact of meeting brethren of like precious faith from the four corners of the earth is a thrilling experience imparting a lasting benefit to the soul. The incipient fanaticism that is rooted in unrecognised pride is sweetly corrected as we mix in the wider circle of others who equally have received the Spirit. All this is within our grasp without the slightest further organisation. As David du Plessis has well said, it is a World Fellowship by recognising – not organising. Finally, we must never forget that unity is a personal matter. When our Lord prayed 'That they all may be one', He meant individual disciples – not denominations and churches. The apostolic exhortations to unity are to personalities. My ultimate unity is with my brother irrespective of whether we belong to the same, or different, outward communions. We do not come together to 'make' unity, for it already exists by the grace of God. It only needs to be cherished. Its test is mutual acceptance of the Lordship of Jesus Christ. Its energy is in the one baptism in the Holy Spirit that He bestows. Its aim is that 'the world may believe'. Its supreme secret is participation in what our Lord called 'the glory'. Lord, send the GLORY! [Gee's capitals]. (*Pentecost*, September 1950)

Thus it was the proposed editorship in 1947 that gave Gee the opportunity to promote these aims in a remarkable way. He performed this new task with obvious zest and relish. Those early years in Edinburgh of training himself to write on a range of topics were now to come to fruition on an international scale, with a continuous flow of lively, informed and influential editorials in the magazine *Pentecost*. An unusual feature of the magazine was that its content

was almost entirely made up of news, reports and many
photographs, but with no individual articles. The only
exception to this was Gee's editorial – a substantial
article on a major theme. In that sense he had the
unique opportunity to be the sole interpretive influence
on the readers of this widely circulated international
magazine, particularly the pastors and leaders of the
movement.

To read these editorials is to encounter Donald Gee
at his best. They show a range and variety of topics,
sometimes critical of Pentecostalism for its narrow-
ness or extremes, sometimes vigorously defending the
tenets of Pentecostalism, especially the value of the
gift of tongues. On other occasions Gee engages non-
Pentecostal church leaders in dialogue, both applaud-
ing and enlarging their comments. He did this notably
with John A. Mackay, President of Princeton Theological Seminary and with Bishop Lesslie Newbigin
of the Church of South India. Similarly he squarely
faces up to the ecumenical movement within the church
and presented outstanding editorials following the
WCC conferences at Amsterdam in 1948, Evanston
in 1954 and New Delhi in 1961. In each of these Gee
sought to chart and guide his fellow Pentecostalists
through these difficult waters. In the end, as we shall
see, Gee was in some of these issues moving too far
ahead for the comfort of the Pentecostal movement
at large.

Whatever one thinks of these editorials, no-one can
fail to appreciate their challenging and stimulating
nature. They gave Gee an unrivalled platform for
Pentecostal statesmanship which he used wisely yet
provocatively in the best editorial manner. The great
contribution which Gee made through this role was
twofold: he exposed Pentecostals to a much wider
range of issues and self-assessment than they normally
engaged in, and for the non-Pentecostal reader he
provided a window on the movement which enabled

them both to understand and to appreciate what God was doing.

To end this chapter on Gee as an international statesman for the Pentecostal movement, the editorial he wrote in *Pentecost* in June 1955, entitled 'Catholic, Protestant and Pentecostal' is reproduced below. It captures some of his best thinking and writing:

Lesslie Newbigin's book *The Household of Faith* reveals that he finds 'three main types of Christianity – the Catholic, the Protestant' and, as he calls it, 'the Pentecostal' laying predominant stress on 'order, faith, and experience' respectively. This penetrating analysis is highly interesting. Mr Newbigin, who is a bishop in the United Church of South India, uses his terms in a typical, and not in a denominational sense, but we who are 'Pentecostal' by designation among the churches can find something well worth examination in this analysis by a theologian of repute. We can accept the proposition that the type of Christianity broadly called 'Pentecostal' emphasizes experience. We plead guilty without apology. We believe that spiritual experience is not only Scriptural but vital to the Christian Gospel. The first Christians had known Jesus personally. They had 'experienced' Jesus Christ. Moreover the Church was born in a mighty experience of the Holy Spirit, made overwhelmingly real by wind and fire and tongues. They experienced a BAPTISM, not a philosophy, of the Spirit. This was far removed from a vague 'receiving by faith without any manifestation', or a mere credal belief that somehow or other all Christians received the Holy Ghost as a matter of form. One of the supreme services that the Pentecostal Movement has rendered to the Church as a whole has been its witness to the *experience* [Gee's italics] of receiving the Spirit.

By allowing room for the gifts of the Spirit
to work and worship, Pentecostal people have
permitted the indwelling Comforter to become
more than a vague Helper or indefinite Inspirer
to virtuous thoughts and high ideals. By incor-
porating Divine healing in their testimony, the
Pentecostal churches include something intensely
experimental. In their fervent evangelism, all
'Pentecostal' groups stress the joy and peace that
come from forgiveness of sins and justification by
faith. The experience of Christian joy is something
essentially Pentecostal (Acts 13: 52). Speaking
with tongues is more than the language of spiritual ecstasy, but it certainly includes that.

The emphasis upon experience can nevertheless
be overdone. The blind man after he was healed by
Jesus said emphatically, 'One thing I know, that
whereas I was blind now I see.' That was glorious.
But after he had received a fuller revelation of
Christ, he worshipped. That revelation was an
experience also, as real as the other, but of a
higher order, for it took him beyond what Christ
had done for him to who Christ was. It took him
away from self to God. The danger of becoming too
experimental in religion is that the soul becomes
introspective, and gets taken up with nothing but
its blessings and feelings and gifts, and therefore
fails in its supreme calling to purely objective
worship of the Living God.

It is, I suppose, Mr Newbigin's meaning, when
he equates the 'Catholic' type of Christianity
with 'order', thus to distinguish those who pre-
dominately stress ritual and liturgical forms of
religious service. Their deadly danger at all times
is formalism. The truly beautiful orders of service
which they evolve end by becoming mechanical
and almost meaningless and powerless for the
majority of their devotees. One of the strange

twists of Church history was that this was the end of the Irvingite (a 'Pentecostal') Movement when it became the Catholic Apostolic Church.

The 'Protestant' type in the analysis [of Mr Newbigin] lays stress on 'faith'. This is the confessional church; the believers for whom what they believe, their doctrines, their creeds, their statement of fundamental dogmas (to which all must subscribe for salvation), are everything. Let us recognise the importance of sound doctrine. Moreover, an intellectual formulation of belief is essential. The danger of the 'Protestant' type of Christianity is that faith enshrined in a creed can become as spiritually sterile as order embalmed in ritual. Succeeding generations cling to a form of words that mean nothing experimentally. It is easy to be impeccably orthodox in faith and to know next to nothing of the abundant life that comes by experiencing Jesus Christ as a Living Saviour.

Must this differentiating 'predominant stress' on order, faith or experience continue to produce different types of Christianity? If there is any truth in the analysis before us, and I believe there is, it indicates the need for the Pentecostal type of church to give more attention to order and to faith. Speaking frankly, it suggests for ourselves within the Pentecostal Revival a need to add to our fervent testimony to experience a greater reverence in worship and a more determined intellectual effort to define our faith.

For many years the intellectual definition of the theological position of the Pentecostal Movement has awaited more adequate attention. This is not asking for a surrender of the Holy Ghost fervour to arid intellectualism. It springs from a pure desire to love and serve God with all our being's ransomed powers, including those of the mind. The three golden strands of order, faith and experience need weaving into one cord that cannot quickly be broken. A Pentecostal Revival in the fullest measure will not stress one at the expense of the other but will manifest a shining witness to all three.

Chapter 13 – Another Springtime

When the 1950s dawned Gee was approaching his sixtieth birthday. The new decade had opened sadly for him with the death of his wife, Ruth. After eighteen years of living at Westgate House in Louth, Lincolnshire where Ruth was the matron of the Pentecostal Women's Bible School run by Howard Carter, they decided to move to a more central location in Bedford. Ruth's health was causing concern and she had already given up her matron's role in the college some years earlier. However, they were only to have a few months together in their new home. Although Donald's travels frequently took him away from the family home, both he and Ruth had been able to journey together to South Africa in the early part of 1950; then sadly at the end of the year, while Donald was preaching in Ireland, Ruth died suddenly.

Those who knew Gee personally recognised the important role Ruth had played in his ministry. She had released him for travel by virtually single-handedly maintaining a stable home and bringing up their three children through the formative years of education. Similarly she had frequently urged and encouraged him in his writing. There is little doubt that without Ruth, he would have achieved far less in many aspects of his talented career.

Despite this clear division of roles within the family and Gee's reserved and shy nature, there was a real affection within the marriage. For some time after

Ruth's death he appeared a sad and lonely figure despite the host of friends and contacts he had made throughout the world. The time that followed could have been his autumn years; but in fact the last fifteen years of his life were to be something of another springtime.

About the time of Ruth's death, the Assemblies of God in Britain were making tentative plans to unite their various independent Bible colleges into one official college at Kenley in Surrey. With remarkable vision they asked Donald Gee to become the first principal. As we shall see, this gave him a new and permanent base for his ongoing ministries as well as exciting opportunities for training the next generation of Pentecostal pastors and leaders.

Similarly at this time the early stirrings of the neo-Pentecostal revival were becoming evident. Gee was to become a focal figure in terms of both response and encouragement towards that new expansion of Pentecostalism. Coupled with this were issues of unity within the Pentecostal movement and the awkward matter of how to relate to the growing ecumenism outside. Gee's experience, status and wisdom drew him into these affairs during the 1950s and 1960s, as we shall see in this chapter.

In 1957 Gee was taken ill while visiting Berlin and was admitted to hospital for examination. The doctor who examined him told him: 'If as soon as you get back to England, you have the major operation that I advise, you will have another springtime.' It appears that Gee needed the removal of the prostate gland; and the operation was later carried out successfully. The phrase 'another springtime' caught Gee's imagination and he used it as the title for his far-reaching chairman's address to the Conference of the British Assemblies of God in 1960. This address is reproduced as Chapter 15 of the present book. Although he used it as an imaginative spur to the pastors and churches in

Britain, it was as we shall see an apt summary of the
final phase of his own ministry. The conference address
caught many of the nuances of his own involvements
and concerns during this period.

The most influential of the events of this era for Gee
was his principalship of the Assemblies of God Bible
School at Kenley. It was during this period that the
present writer came to know Gee personally, studying
under him for a time during 1959–60. From its earliest days the Pentecostal movement in Britain had
established Bible training colleges. In 1910 Thomas
Myerscough at Preston had become principal of a school
for training Pentecostal missionaries and evangelists
in conjunction with the Pentecostal Missionary Union.
In this school men such as George Jeffreys and William
Burton were students. At the same time Cecil Polhill,
the leader of the Pentecostal Missionary Union, opened
a London college along similar lines with two separate
locations – one for men, the other for women. After
World War I the men's college in Hampstead reopened
under the principalship of Howard Carter; the women's
college moved to Louth, where eventually Ruth Gee
was to become matron. When the Assemblies of God
were formed in Britain in 1924, Carter's school, though
independent, was in associate membership with the
new movement. To all intents and purposes it was the
unofficial Assemblies of God Bible College. Carter's
undoubted teaching skills, together with his emphasis
on faith, led to the pioneering of several new assemblies
in the 1930s and the training of his students to pastor
the new churches.

In 1947 another independent Assemblies of God
college opened in Bristol under the leadership of John
Wallace. Then surprisingly in the following year Carter
decided to relinquish the long-held principalship of the
Hampstead school. Carter was not due for retirement
at that time. Born in the same year as Gee, he was in
his late fifties. But he was growing older, and as well as

wanting the freedom to travel, he wanted to hand over
his heavy responsibilities to a younger man, a capable
administrator and teacher named George Newsholme.
However with the personality of Carter no longer an
attraction the number of students began to drop. Thus
many within the Assemblies of God began to think
of a fresh start and a more official college for the
denomination.

Newsholme had already begun to look for new premises, and found an attractive building in Surrey at
Kenley, a few miles south of Croydon. It was set in
pleasant grounds with large lawns and some scope for
expansion. Originally it had been a private house but
was now a small hotel. Both Newsholme and Wallace
were happy to merge their colleges and then hand
over responsibility to the Assemblies of God. Thus the
premises in Kenley were purchased. In 1951 a Board
of Governors was created which recommended Donald
Gee's appointment as the first principal.

To the surprise of many – because Gee was more of
a field-teacher than a cloistered academic and because
he was extremely busy with his international ministry
and editorial work – he accepted. Gee remained there
for thirteen reasonably happy years, retiring in his
early seventies. Although on first sight his appointment seemed unlikely, in many ways the situation
suited him well. It gave him a new home after his wife's
death and, from a psychological point of view in the
post-bereavement period, some revitalising new inter-
ests and challenges. His existing work fitted in quite
well with college life; he continued to edit *Pentecost*
from his small study overlooking the delightful rear
lawns of the college, and the vacations left him free to
travel as widely as he wished; the travel facilities of
London were close at hand. The financial remuneration
from Gee's itinerant ministry enabled him to refuse a
salary throughout his time as principal.

Even Gee himself found his appointment a little

surprising, because he had never been to a theological college and like many self-made men, tended to feel such training unnecessary. He wrote later on recognising that attitude:

Bible Schools are unnecessary. That is exactly what I used to say for many years; and I believed it too! It is a fitting revenge that in the providence of God I now find myself principal of such an institution. What made me talk like that? ... Looking back, I now know that in my case there was an unrecognised tincture of pride in what I said. I foolishly felt that I was doing pretty well as a pastor and later as a writer of sorts, and then a world traveller. In my heart I was saying, 'See what I have done without going to any Bible School.' (*Redemption Tidings*, February 1958)

The courses lasted for two years and Gee's characteristic sign-writer's signature, which had become something of a personal logo, went on to each diploma awarded. The syllabus was fairly standard material for most evangelical colleges of that era, with an emphasis on the Bible books, doctrine and evangelism, but understood from a Pentecostal perspective. Gee's own lectures were on Pentecostal doctrine, such as the gifts of the Holy Spirit, and church history, majoring on the Pentecostal movement. His style of lecturing, like that of his writing, was clear and logical; only his gruff, bell-like diction and puckish sense of humour made one see the personality beyond his writings.

Also, he gave courses on pastoral theology, where his rich experience could hold full sway. Many felt that Gee was at his best in these courses, talking with all his common-sense and balance to future pastors about such issues as the trials of a young pastor, the value of private study and how to conduct a whole range of

public meetings and services. Gee was quite flexible
and imaginative in his teaching and in the summer
months would sometimes take the class out on to
the lawns. There he would throw out a topic for open
discussion, encouraging the class to think through such
issues as: What is the difference between heresy and
divisiveness in an assembly and how does one deal with
such situations? Here he drew on some of his early
experiences where his own pastor, A.E. Saxby, began
to espouse the view of universalism; similarly in his
first pastorate in Leith where some were attracted to
extreme Pentecostal practices and caused Gee almost
to abandon his work.

The following is a paraphrase of one such lecture
given by Gee on the interesting topic 'How to conduct a
waiting meeting for the baptism in the Holy Spirit':

We must first of all realise that God is sovereign
in these matters and may baptise us in a number
of forms and circumstances. It is good however
to have special occasions for waiting upon God.
There is a benefit in regular waiting meetings in
an assembly, as regular as prayer meetings, then
people can not only pray to be baptised in the Holy
Spirit, but to be re-filled also. The Pentecostal
revival was born in waiting meetings and not in
campaigns. It will die as a revival if these meetings
are left off. The aim of these meetings is to seek
the fulness of the Spirit and not for intercession.
They must have a definite aim and be restricted
in invitation. Only those of one accord and one
heart should attend. There must be no spectators
or novelty-seekers. As well it should be unhurried
in time because it is waiting upon God. People can
leave when they like and the meeting will finish
when God wills it. In order to fit such waiting
meetings in, some surgery may be needed in
an overcrowded church programme. The leader's

part first of all relates to concentration. He must help people to have a definite aim. Well chosen hymns and a brief sermon of exhortation are valuable. Moreover he must arrange for physical comfort in the meeting. There is no need for kneeling all the time, people can sit or stand or be provided with kneeling mats. So long as they can concentrate. Next the leader must encourage faith. Be personally free and others will follow. Praise helps faith. Faith is contagious, so let people be infected by you. Faith must always say : now! The laying-on of hands can be a major help to faith. However encourage the 'rest of faith'. There is a tendency to strain and struggle; shouting and jumping does not necessarily help faith. Therefore speaking with tongues should be spontaneous and not forced. It is the leader's role to restrain the flesh. This needs great wisdom; we need the gift of governments. There must be a responsible leader, there is danger in groups just gathering among themselves. However remember that the Holy Spirit's manifestation may not always fit our natural mind or trend or tradition or taste. The leader must be cautious before stopping or preventing any activities. If matters are getting a little out of hand, read an appropriate scripture or ask the people to sing a hymn and then continue to pray. Finally we must watch against evil spirits. The greatest blessings and greatest difficulties sometimes come together. Satan always comes to waiting meetings! But do not be afraid in these matters – for fear is as contagious as faith.

Gee did not have to involve himself greatly in the administration of the college. This was in the hands of the dean, Elisha Thompson, who with the help of a secretary maintained the day-to-day running of the college. Thompson was the only residential

tutor, apart from Gee himself. Others were drawn
from the headquarters staff of the Assemblies of God
in London and came for one day each week. They were
John Carter, the General Secretary, Leslie Woodford,
the Missionary Secretary and Aaron Lindford the
editor of *Redemption Tidings*. Later on Alfred Missen,
successor to John Carter, also lectured. Other visiting
lecturers came, especially men like W.T.H. Richards,
from Slough with energetic pastoral and evangelistic skills.

All these men were capable teachers and gave the
students a contact with all the major departments of
Assemblies of God. It would seem that Gee and his governors were determined that the college should reflect
its official status within the denomination. The only
exception to this was C.L. Parker. He had lectured in
Carter's Hampstead college and was an unusual character within British Pentecostalism, being a former
Anglican clergyman and an Oxford don with a degree
in classics. Because of his wide biblical knowledge
and lecturing flair, Carter had tended to overlook
some of his doctrinal idiosyncrasies. For example,
Parker felt that some unsaved people may well have
an opportunity to hear the gospel after death – the
so-called 'second chance' teaching. However, now that
the college was subject to the Assemblies of God
ministers' conference, the issue was formally raised
and Parker forced to resign in 1956. It is interesting that the issue was raised by sections within
the conference and not by Gee himself as principal. There is little doubt that Gee disagreed with
Parker's specific teaching on this matter, but was
wise enough to try to retain a man of such abilities within the college until the conference ruled
otherwise.

The students who enrolled at the college were generally training for pastoral ministry within the British Assemblies of God. Others were intending to be

overseas missionaries, especially in the main Assemblies of God field in Zaire. Gee's presence attracted a number from overseas, particularly from countries he visited regularly such as Holland, France, Germany and Switzerland. Many of these countries did not as yet have their own Pentecostal colleges.

During Gee's time at Kenley the work was a steadily growing success. When he began in 1951 the number of students was eighteen but within two years the total had doubled and a debt of £3,500 on the property had been paid off. As 1960 approached it became necessary to build an annexe and then a few years later another floor above it. Student numbers were now at capacity at around sixty men and women. He encouraged evangelism and open-air ministry in nearby Croydon, and above all sought to maintain the spiritual glow of the college by monthly days of prayer. A wide range of weekend preaching opportunities came into the college for students to fulfil and Gee himself often took parties out to churches, especially using some of the talented singing groups which developed.

One of his most valuable initiatives involved the bringing together of the four main Pentecostal Bible Colleges for a united witness meeting, often held in Spurgeon's Tabernacle in south London. The colleges involved were Elim at Clapham, the Apostolic Church at Penygroes in south Wales, the International Bible Training Institute at Burgess Hill in Sussex and Kenley itself. Gee's instinct for unity among Pentecostals in Britain caused him to see the value of future leaders meeting together in their formative years of training.

Of course Gee had his idiosyncrasies. He insisted on half-an-hour of total quiet throughout the college immediately after lunch so that he and others could rest. Students had to personally provide their own linen serviettes which Gee insisted should be set out at all meals, whether they were used or not.

This was slightly strange considering that most of his students were from a working-class background! Similarly, because he had been personally involved in the production of a series of Pentecostal hymn books, and because he knew that assemblies only sang their favourite hymns, he insisted that the college should progressively sing its way through Redemption Hymnal at the short time of worship following breakfast. This meant that hymns for various seasons of the year, or special occasions such as weddings and funerals, would be sung out of season if that section of the book had been reached. At times he could be quite caustic in his comments about the musical abilities of students.

Some found him aloof and censorious. On the other hand for a man of Gee's age, experience and indeed basic shyness it must have been very difficult living with fifty exuberant and often gauche students. The fact that he accomplished this for thirteen years, without any major problems, is a further insight into his character.

In trying to assess this period in Gee's ministry most would recognise that Gee brought status and credibility to the new college. His wide experience and international reputation ensured that. In addition his work gave similar value to the British Assemblies of God themselves. The American Pentecostals had developed their Bible colleges more effectively and Britain had been looked on as being small-minded in its planning and rather parochial in its methods. Now its national college presented another, more positive image, especially with Gee as principal.

In addition Gee made Bible college training more acceptable within a movement where many still thought that the anointing of the Spirit was the only preparation that was needed for ministry – which, as we have already seen, was partly Gee's own attitude at one time. In that same article quoted earlier, Gee continued to give some reasons why he and others mistakenly thought in that way. He noted:

> More solid ground for saying that Bible Schools were unnecessary was the fact that among my colleagues in those pioneering days of the Pentecostal Movement were several rugged old pioneers who, like myself, had never been to any Bible School, but were doing solid work for God. They were however men of strong natural intelligence and ability. Moreover the baptism in the Spirit had given them such a passionate love for the Bible that it would hardly be too much to affirm that in certain aspects of scriptural knowledge in which they specialised they became true scholars. If they were self-taught, they were certainly not ill-taught. But they were exceptional men, doing exceptional work. Truth requires us to admit that alongside them there were scores of other men who accomplished little through sheer lack of ability. (*Redemption Tidings*, February 1958)

Hence Gee played a major part within the Pentecostal movement in encouraging formal theological training as a necessary part of preparing for Pentecostal ministry. Pioneering pastors and a more competent ministry of the Bible were evidences of the success of Gee's emphasis within the Assemblies of God. Even evangelists found encouragement rather than a stifling of their gifts at Kenley, as witnessed by the successful ministry of the Dutch evangelist Hans Koornstra who studied there in the early 1960s.

Of course Gee recognised some of the dangers too. On one occasion he wrote perceptively about what he saw for Spirit-filled students as 'The perils of Bible Schools'. Among these he included *prayerlessness*; living in a crowded, busy college can make time alone

with God difficult to maintain. Secondly, *professional-
ism* can begin to creep in to one's ministry. An emphasis upon knowledge and technique can obscure experience and spiritual gifting. Gee was anxious that spiritual growth and maturity should not be lost or reduced
to a secondary place in the training programme. Lastly
he warned against *pride and false status* through
having attended a ministerial Bible college; rather
he felt that being part of such a college should be a
humbling experience of recognising one's inadequacies
and a greater need for the Holy Spirit's power.

Over all, the mark which Gee impressed upon the
college was training that was solid and perhaps more
straightforward than Howard Carter's individualistic
approach. There was Gee's characteristic emphasis on
balance and the cautious questioning of the fanatical
or superficial aspects of Pentecostal practices. This led
some less-discerning pastors within the Assemblies
of God to accuse Gee of quenching, by his methods,
the fervour of some of the young men who entered
the college. However that reaction appears to have
been merely the ongoing battle that Gee fought all
his life as he tried to establish the true place of the
teacher, as well as the prophet, within the Pentecostal
movement.

From a personal point of view the present writer
remembers most vividly, from Gee's era as principal,
the regular stream of visitors to the college who were
drawn there by Gee's presence. This enabled students
to meet a range of international Pentecostal leaders in
a most remarkable way. On one occasion many members of the planning committee for a Pentecostal World
Conference were at Kenley and one met such figures
as Thomas Zimmerman, the General Superintendent of
the American Assemblies of God. Then Teddy Hodgson,
a veteran missionary from Zaire, was staying with Gee
a few months before his martyrdom during the uprising
in Zaire in 1960. The writer well remembers the last

embrace Gee gave Hodgson when he interrupted one of Gee's lectures in order to say farewell. Equally vivid is the memory of Gee with tears in his eyes, announcing shortly afterwards to the student body that Hodgson had been killed protecting a younger missionary.

Perhaps the most startling of all Gee's visitors was David du Plessis. Gee felt that what he had to share should be heard by all the students present in 1960. There, with a measure of incredulity, du Plessis was heard telling of remarkable happenings in the historic denominational churches of America where Episcopalians were speaking in tongues and what we now know as the charismatic renewal movement was beginning. Du Plessis also shared something of his own testimony, beginning with the prophecy which Smith Wigglesworth had given to him; that he would be involved in precisely such a widening of the Pentecostal experience.

It may well be that for many students it was such meetings and events, focused around Gee's own personality and international role, which gave to them and the college an indefinable extra significance.

Gee began to plan for his retirement from Kenley when he celebrated his seventieth birthday in 1961. In the end, through little fault of his own, the actual process was rather a messy one. The General Conference of Assemblies of God in 1962 unanimously appointed him for a final two years as principal. During the following year, in anticipation of that retirement, the college governors had recommended a successor, Robert Barrie. For reasons that are still not quite clear, the General Conference was not prepared to accept Barrie's nomination at that time, although later on he did become the college principal. As often happens in those kinds of conference discussions, issues were raised about the efficient running of the college, which Gee took personally. Meanwhile others were suggesting that he could be

too old, and his health not good enough, for such a
key position.

In the light of these disagreements over finding a
successor to Gee and the likelihood that he might be
asked to stay on for a further year, one of the college
staff, Ernest Crewe, wrote in protest to the governors.
Crewe pointed out that those closest to Gee could see
that 'he really is not physically fit enough to carry the
burden for another term of office'.

Gee's usual insight and wisdom, perhaps because of
these tensions, failed him. Despite the fact that his
doctor had diagnosed hardening of the arteries and
rising blood pressure, he suggested that his health
was not too bad. His advice to the governors was to
continue looking for a successor, but 'without treating
the matter as urgent'. He even went so far as to
suggest that the long-standing dean of the college,
Elisha Thompson, should be offered the post. However
in the 1964 General Conference, Thompson failed to
be elected and the governors once more presented the
name of Robert Barrie. This time Barrie was voted in
and Gee duly retired from office as principal at the age
of seventy-three.

Unfortunately the saga did not quite end there. It
would seem that a combination of lack of forward
planning by the Assemblies of God and the touchiness
of Gee's character led to further frustrations. Gee had
no home to which to retire, and the Assemblies of God
could only give him a modest retirement gift and a
small pension. He was eventually offered by his friend
Jean Wildrianne, the principal of the International
Bible Teaching Institute in Sussex, a room in the
Institute where he could both live and undertake some
lecturing. However, Gee had other plans and solutions
to his situation. To the surprise of many, having been a
widower for fourteen years he was to remarry within a
few months of leaving Kenley, and the closing years of
his life were to be enriched by this new partnership.

Nevertheless despite these various issues Gee was given a special tribute at the 1965 Conference for his service as college principal, revealing the deep-seated affection which the denomination held for him. Part of the written tribute given to him said:

> We also recognise the benefit which our college has reaped through your world reputation as a gifted author and Bible teacher. May you be spared for many years to serve our Lord and to assist still further the Pentecostal movement by your pen and preaching.

Sadly this was not to be the case. Just over a year after those sentiments being expressed, Gee was dead. However there is one last area in Gee's second springtime which must be considered before we come to those final months of his life; his involvement with the emerging neo-Pentecostal movement within the historic churches.

Chapter 14 – Charismatic Renewal

It has already become clear that Gee was much bigger than one denomination as, indeed, he was bigger than one country. During the last fifteen years of his life he devoted considerable energy to encouraging Pentecostals in Britain and worldwide to work more closely together. Later this was to include the historic Protestant and Catholic churches as well, when they began to share in the charismatic renewal. Remarkably, for a short while, Gee was even prepared to open unofficial links with the World Council of Churches alongside the efforts of David du Plessis.

In Gee's book *Toward Pentecostal Unity* which first appeared in 1961, the publisher's foreword states:

> Near the end of his long preaching and writing ministry within the Pentecostal Movement, Donald Gee could visualize no worldwide denomination to embrace all Pentecostals. He was certain that organizational unity was an impossible dream. His vision and prayer, however, was that Pentecostals would drop petty differences and independent attitudes and then unite in spirit and various ways to evangelise the world. He called for 'a world fellowship by recognizing – not organising'.

Both in that book and as we have seen in the editorial

articles of *Pentecost*, Gee sought to realise something of this dream. His method was not to dilute Pentecostalism in order to gain this goal but to strongly affirm that the central beliefs and experiences were above the various issues which originally created the different groups. It is exhilarating to read some of his chapters on such themes as, 'I believe in the Holy Ghost' and 'Do Tongues Matter?'

Some of Gee's thinking had been coloured by a vision a missionary friend had seen during a conference Gee had attended with him in South Africa. The incident is recalled in one of the early chapters of the book despite the fact that Gee was usually 'chary of printing reports of visions and prophecies.' The man had written:

I wonder if you still remember a vision the Lord gave me at that first United Pentecostal Missionary Conference in Johannesburg when you were out here? In that vision a large congregation of Christian workers could be seen, all looking forward, towards a platform where Jesus was standing. While they could all see the platform they could not see each other because there were wooden partitions around each person, so that none could have fellowship with the others. But it was clear they all had the same aim and that all were looking to Christ. Then a wonderful quiet fire came down from heaven, going through these wooden partitions which burnt up in that fire, but no smoke or flames could be seen and it did not disturb the people. The partitions just seemed to burn up and disappear. And now the workers could see each other and greeted each other and there seemed to be such wonderful harmony and they continued looking forward to Christ who was still standing on the platform. Although the wooden partitions had disappeared, it did not alter the position of the various workers;

each one still kept his own individuality, but they all seemed to love each other and to esteem each other highly.

Gee interpreted and applied this vision in terms of united evangelism. He went on to comment:

We *are* [Gee's italics] seeing all over the world, the fulfilment of the vision. Those who want to maintain or rebuild the partitions should be very careful lest haply they work against God. Especially mistaken are any zealots trying to build up a new Pentecostal body, hoping thereby to absorb all the others. They never will; but it would be amusing if it were not pathetic to observe how blind new movements can be to the plain fact that their divisive tactics, often covered with much mouthing of 'unity' are only heading for the creation of just one more little sect . . . When the church devotes herself to her supreme business of evangelism she finds as a blessed by-product a spontaneous unity bursting through all her sections. A genuine love for souls carries with it a love for the brethren also. We justly look with doubtfulness upon a boasted zeal for evangelism that makes men narrow, bigoted and censorious . . . It is time to burn our partitions, not one another.

This concern for worldwide unity of purpose which Gee was encouraging showed itself at the local level when he was one of the prime movers in bringing about the formation of the British Pentecostal Fellowship in 1948. Together with four other main Pentecostal groups in Britain, Gee had been one of the Assemblies of God leaders who met for a two-day conference in London to explore the idea of closer cooperation. The main result of this new accord was not so much joint efforts but a greater appreciation of one another and less suspicion between the denominations. Sadly George Jeffrey's Bible Pattern Fellowship quickly dropped out of the original group.

At the time that these endeavours by Gee towards local and worldwide co-operation of Pentecostals were happening, a more significant change was taking place. The Pentecostal experience was occurring within the historic churches and the charismatic renewal movement was underway. Now the Pentecostal churches not only had to define their attitudes towards each other but also to the denominations which had once shunned them. In characteristic fashion Gee was to play a part in these matters.

In the final chapter of his Pentecostal history, completed just before his death in 1966, Gee gives a positive and encouraging account of what he called 'Pentecost outside "Pentecost"', the neo-Pentecostal movement. Despite the caution of other leaders he recognised du Plessis' unusual role as a Pentecostal ambassador to the wider church and described him not as some were doing as a 'Pentecostal ecumaniac', but rather as 'a man of God for the hour'. Similarly in the magazine *Pentecost* Gee gave regular space to accounts of du Plessis' activities. Nevertheless he was perceptive enough to see that the coming of the new Pentecostalism of the charismatic renewal movement in the 1960s did not necessarily mean the end of the old classical Pentecostalism. Rather, they should enrich one another.

Sometimes in the nature of two rivers, when they unite, flow side by side for a time before the waters completely mingle. When the Lord began to work in Pentecostal grace among the older denominations there were some who spoke disparagingly of the older existing Pentecostal Movement as though it were a spent force that had been discarded by the Spirit of God. The facts emphatically disprove this view. (*Wind and Flame*)

On the other hand Gee was perceptive enough to see that the new groups should not necessarily leave their existing denominations to join the classical Pentecostal groupings or even form new denominations.

As early as 1953 he had written an editorial in *Pentecost* warning of this when occasionally individuals from other churches were being baptised in the Holy Spirit. He observed:

> Let us beware of making it our supreme aim to drag people into our own denomination. If they can maintain unsullied and intact their Pentecostal witness where they are, then let them do it. Our experience causes us to expect that they will have difficulty. Our hope is that such difficulty will grow less as truth wins certain victories. Our prayer will henceforth be that the floodtide of Pentecostal grace and power that should follow speaking with tongues may be manifested in any and all of the churches, for Pentecost is more than a denomination; it is a REVIVAL [Gee's capitals]. (*Pentecost*, September 1953)

There seems to be plenty of evidence that from the beginning of the neo-Pentecostal movement in the early 1960s Gee welcomed it and recognised it as a new move of God in a wider Pentecostal revival. In his own writings he says little of his own personal involvement, but the researches of Peter Hocken published in *Streams of Renewal – The Origins and Early Development of the Charismatic Movement in Great Britain* (Exeter 1986), reveal some fascinating material. Once more Gee is shown to be a remarkable and farsighted Pentecostal statesman.

Gee's involvement came about through his growing friendship with David du Plessis. In many ways Gee's part in the charismatic renewal movement was to be supportive of du Plessis and therefore in a sense secondary, but nevertheless because of his enormous personal influence, significant.

Du Plessis and Gee went together as observers to the meeting of the Faith and Order Commission of the World Council of Churches at St Andrews in Scotland in 1960. Many leading British churchmen, including Archbishop Michael Ramsey and prominent Roman Catholic observers were at this meeting and heard du Plessis' address describing the unusual Pentecostal developments within the historic churches.

This partnership would have continued in the much larger arena of the conference of the World Council of Churches at New Delhi in 1961 to which Gee and du Plessis had been invited. However the British and American Assemblies of God put pressure on Gee not to attend. They felt that it might hinder the developing relations between them and the wider evangelical churches who were suspicious of the more liberal ecumenical movement. So du Plessis carried on this open involvement whereas Gee adopted a more distant and supportive role. Hocken notes:

> While du Plessis was actively promoting this new work outside the Pentecostal ranks, Gee was defending him and striving to open Pentecostal minds and hearts to this unexpected blessing. (*Streams of Renewal*)

Further on he again depicts Gee's significant role in these events. He observed:

> In his mission, du Plessis was supported by Donald Gee, whose writings provided intellectual grounds

for positions du Plessis arrived at more instinctively. Gee, with his knowledge of Pentecostal history, was able to contrast the reaction of the churches to the early Pentecostal movement in the first decade of the century with the reaction of the same churches to the 'new wave' some five to six decades later. (*Streams of Renewal*)

However, this is not the whole story of Gee's involvement. Behind the scenes Gee had developed a remarkable friendship and correspondence with a Roman Catholic priest, Dom Benedict Heron from Belgium. Hocken suggests that when they first met in London, Gee may well have thought that Heron was an Anglican clergyman, but discovering the true identity of his colleague did not deter Gee from inviting him to Kenley in 1960. From that first visit right to Gee's death in 1966 they maintained contact by correspondence and personal meetings.

The following letter from Gee to Heron in June 1960 was among the earlier stages of that correspondence, and gives a fascinating insight into Gee's thinking and visions:

It has given me very great joy to receive your kind letter of June 11. I have often thought of our afternoon of fellowship last winter, and have been touched at the thought of you going to the trouble to make the long journey to Kenley especially to make this possible.

I am more convinced than ever of the essential unity of those truly in Christ Jesus, even when members of communions as utterly diverse as Roman Catholic and Pentecostal. This is really an amazing thing, perhaps more of a 'miracle' than some of the things we mutually call 'miracles'.

You have enriched my own spiritual life very much
by this gesture of love and fellowship. In the
Pentecostal Movement I am trying to inculcate a
bigger vision in many ways, and I am sure that the
atmosphere is changing in that direction. In both
the Roman Catholic and the Pentecostal groups
there are extremists which we must both deplore.
I fear there are some among us who almost
equate 'Protestant' with 'Christian', and there
is almost as much ignorance and prejudice where
the Orthodox Churches are concerned. It is my
privilege to teach Church History to the students
here, and so I have some golden opportunities to
inculcate a more balanced view. But my need of
carefulness has to be as great as your own, and
I know you will treat this letter with the same
great discretion that I accord yours.

I read the pamphlet about the Abbe Paul Cou-
turier that you kindly left with me with great
appreciation. Such are the true saints of THE
CHURCH. [Gee's capitals]. I would like you to
attend a really good Pentecostal meeting, but I
fear there are many that I hesitate to commend
to such as yourself because of their weaknesses.
And yet the Holy Spirit is greater than Pentecostal
meetings when the manifestations of the Holy
Spirit are in evidence. There are some Pentecostal
meetings in Belgium, but I have not visited them
personally. Let us believe that the Lord will open
this for you in His Own best time and way.

There is a constant temptation to imitation
when we profess belief in the present miraculous.
Some sincerely confuse the psychic. Also I think
we need to be careful in our definitions. Among
Pentecostals the term 'supernatural' is used much
too loosely. In many it just means the spectacular.
We need to see the grace and power of God at work
in ways not so immediately spectacular. How good

if and when we can mutually come together to talk about these things. For the glory of God. I hope you will feel free to keep in touch with me, and please accept again my assurance of how deeply I value this fellowship in Christ.

For Gee, his principalship of the Bible College and involvement with the emerging charismatic renewal movement were all fulfilment of the promise of 'another springtime'. The final period of his life must soon be described, but first let us return to his important address given to the British Assemblies of God Conference in 1960 and see how all of these strands and themes are taken up in characteristic style by him along with other issues.

In this we will catch the authentic flavour of the man at his best, before completing the account of those final days where spring eventually gave way to autumn.

Chapter 15 – Challenge
to the Movement

ANOTHER SPRINGTIME –
1960 Conference Address

The Scripture with which I wish to begin my message is found in Psalm 110, verse 3 – 'Thy people shall be willing in the day of Thy power, in the beauties of holiness from the womb of the morning; Thou hast the dew of Thy youth.' Especially that last phrase.

The title of my message is 'Another Springtime'. It has been born out of the deep water of an experience I was permitted to go through in the autumn of 1957, and I ask your forgiveness for the personal allusion. While ministering in Berlin a physical weakness came to a head and I collapsed. My hosts rushed me into hospital against my will. While there the German surgeon said to me – 'If, as soon as you get back to England, you have the major operation that I advise you will have another springtime, but if not you will die.' I decided to have the operation. It was successful, and by the goodness of God I think I can gratefully say that He is giving me to taste another 'springtime' in my physical health.

The words of that German surgeon have lived with me, and I have become increasingly convinced that they should provide the key-note of my message to this General Conference of

Assemblies of God in Great Britain and Ireland in 1960, for I believe that by the grace of God our beloved Fellowship of Pentecostal churches can enjoy another spiritual springtime. But it may necessitate an act of divine surgery.

It is obvious that my message demands that I ask you to face with me some challenging questions. Do we need another spiritual springtime? Is such a thing possible? Can we do anything to forward it and if so what? Are there any signs that it has already begun?

I shall not labour the question that some new breath of revival is needed, for the expressions of longing for this are too deep and universal to be insignificant. To offer you a shallow optimism when spiritual surgery may be needed is to be unfaithful to a sacred trust. Yet a diagnosis of our spiritual condition needs to be made with very great care.

First of all let us look with joy at the grace of God among us. Our great conventions all over the British Isles are occasions of heart-stirring grace and glory. In them, in our evangelistic campaigns, in our youth rallies, and best of all in our hundreds of local assemblies, there is a continuous stream of conversions and baptisms in the Holy Spirit, and testimonies to divine healing. Our Fellowship is still full of missionary zeal and our offerings for missionary work are touching a record level. Our achievement as a small denomination in keeping 'Revivaltime' on the air for four and a half years at a cost of about £120 per week was an amazing feat. A number of our churches have erected or acquired in recent months and years valuable properties of modern design with excellent amenities for carrying on an aggressive work in the Gospel. God has given us at Kenley a Bible College of which any denomination might be proud that has been packed to the doors with keen young students for over eight years, and has recently been enlarged. Our Sunday School work is steadily increasing, and many assemblies now have branch schools to fulfil their zeal in this vital matter. Evangelism in all its forms is engaging our constant attention and not least our new zeal for doorbell evangelism. Should the title of my message recall the tag from Shelley, 'If winter comes can spring be far behind?' then we can only describe it as a truly glorious winter, bright with heavenly sunshine and the envy of less-favoured spiritual climes. If this be 'winter', then what will the following springtime be like!

Yet honesty compels us to face symptoms not so happy. We are concerned at the slowness of our numerical growth. It is true that the number of assemblies is creeping up year by year, but it is only creeping when we want it to be leaping. This slowness of growth of the Pentecostal Movement in the British Isles in comparison with other countries is the subject of frequent discussion among us, and rightly so. Nobody seems to have a completely satisfactory answer. We cannot exclude the sovereignty of God while we wait for Him to be gracious.

Of special concern are those little assemblies here and there that are visibly dying. They are living in the past. God forbid that we should despise faithfulness, but our souls cannot live on tradition. Jesus taught that the husbandman is drastic with fruitlessness in Christ. Dead wood has to be cut away and divine surgery is His method to produce a new burst of fruit-bearing. Assemblies cannot expect to be fruitful unless they provide in Christ a living ministry of the word and the Spirit. Sheer incompetency on our platforms is never Pentecostal. It must be cut out.

Of almost equal concern are misguided folk who
turn to artificially produced emotionalism as a
substitute for a genuine work of the Holy Spirit.
Those who have known the true, refuse to be carried away by such substitutes for genuine revival,
but the unwary can be deceived. It is impossible
to find lasting satisfaction without a ministry of
the word. Even a self-confessed dryness is better
than administering false stimulants to a thirsty
soul that leave it worse than ever.

A few months ago, in preparing them for publication, I read through once more the three
conference messages of John Wallace in 1950,
1954 and 1958. As we read those impassioned
utterances now we feel again that authentic note
of prophetic authority we were conscious of as
many of us heard them in Morecambe, Hopton
and Skegness. They are weighty with the burden
of the Lord upon a soul that had personally
tasted, though somewhat late in time, the first
springtime of this revival in the early 1920s, and
felt that we were losing the freshness and depth
of those formative years. They are full of warning
against backsliding. But let us remember that the
Spirit of God gives prophecy in the churches for
exhortation, edification and comfort. Where we
need to repent, we can repent. When God speaks
we can have ears to hear. If we are challenged
to action we can accept the challenge and yield
obedience to Jesus Christ as Lord. I stand here
today to declare that John Wallace, now taken
from us, need not have spoken in vain.

But, secondly, is another 'springtime' possible
for Assemblies of God? There is a fatalistic interpretation of church history that affirms that all
revival movements must pass through fixed stages
of rise, maturity and decay until at last they
become something like an extinct volcano. The

mountain remains in the form of just another denomination, but the fire has gone. We must face such a possibility for ourselves. There is considerable historical support for the view, but thank God the evidence is neither complete nor conclusive. There are churches and believers in some of the older denominations that are burning and shining for Christ.

We too, have become a denomination of over 500 churches, linked in spiritual fellowship with much larger groups all over the world bearing the same or similar name. There are believers to whom the very word 'denomination' is abhorrent. They immediately connect it with that which is inimical to revival. They need to think again, and think more deeply. The springs of spiritual revivals go far deeper than mere denominational association – or lack of it. Those who cannot work within some recognized denomination need to look well and deeply into their own hearts for the reason.

But to go more carefully into this vital question of whether, or not, we can have another springtime in the Pentecostal churches I turn to the text with which I began, and especially that last phrase concerning the Messiah: 'Thou hast the dew of Thy youth'. It has sometimes been said that since our Redeemer finished His work on earth, and ascended back to the Father, by the time He was only thirty-three years of age He took to heaven a human body in all its early bloom of maturity. One writer has described Him as 'The Young Prince of Glory'. His eternal Sonship knows no age, and His glory was shared with the Father before the world was. Dare I make the application of these sublime truths to the matter in hand and say that in the Spirit of Christ there can be neither age or decay. If we are filled with His Spirit, and if we follow Him, we shall participate in that everlasting dew of His youth. In Christ we shall be young for ever.

Do not misunderstand me. I am making no plea for fanatical ideas regarding the physical frame in which the Bible says we sometimes groan 'earnestly desiring to be clothed upon with our house that is from heaven'. But we go on to read that 'though our outward man perish, yet the inward man is renewed day by day'. There need be no ageing of the spiritual life, only a maturing and a developing. If it be replied that all this is for personal application only I will make bold to say that the churches are made up of companies of individuals, and if enough of them keep filled with the Spirit then whole churches and whole groups of churches, can unitedly enjoy the secret source of perpetual spiritual youth. Denominations cannot be revived as such, but individuals can, and denominations are only aggregates of individuals. The ultimate issue is personal.

We accept the fact that historically the first springtime of the Pentecostal Movement has passed. In the early decades of this heaven-sent revival there was a thrill of sheer novelty that, in the exquisite words of our text, had the 'beauties of holiness from the womb of the morning'. That thrill is enjoyed still by thousands as they enter into their individual heritage of the baptism in the Holy Spirit and speak with tongues as the Spirit gives them utterance. But in those early years of the movement, and I speak as one of the rapidly decreasing number who shared in them, we were all 'Pentecostally' young together. In the realm of spiritual gifts, particularly, we were pioneering. We made mistakes, but it was exciting and exhilarating, though sometimes dangerous. Not all survived. But those who have should be able, by God's grace, to give spiritual leadership to the second and third generations now pressing forward. We ought to be, and I humbly believe we are, equipped by the new Spirit for a new move in God. I cannot believe that the Lord wants this ability for matured spiritual leadership wasted. Within another springtime there is work to be done.

But to declare a faith like this places upon us a responsibility to be constructive. Therefore our third and crucial question asks if there is anything we can do to work with God in forwarding another springtime. I hold that all revivals are subject to the sovereignty of God, but beliefs in the sovereignty of God in any sphere of theology must never become fatalism. In healthy souls it never does. What can we do, therefore? To what operations of spiritual surgery can we submit? Wishful thinking is not enough. Pious platitudes and sighings for revival are not enough. Even praying by itself, is not enough. Work must go with prayer.

My first suggestion may appear superficial. I hope it is not too revolutionary. But it is my humble opinion that our Constitutional Minutes need to be entirely revised and brought up to date. They were framed over 35 years ago in an endeavour to meet the clamant need of about seventy little independent Pentecostal assemblies that wanted protection against heresy and fanaticism, but were terrified of sacrificing anything of their local autonomy. There is nothing sacrosanct about our Constitution, and as one who helped frame it I think I have the right to make the disclaimer. It has been added to and patched up so much through the years that it almost needs a trained lawyer to follow all its ramifications and cross-references. I realize that by itself such an act of denominational surgery cannot lead to a renewed revival, but I am persuaded that it would inspire that feeling of a new beginning which we badly need. The revision that I have in mind would leave inviolate the truly fundamental principles of our faith and practice. I will now turn to much deeper matters, but let us face the fact that for good or ill our Constitution is the organizational framework which we have devised for ourselves to work in and by. Let us seek the very best.

My second suggestion takes us much deeper. I am convinced that bigger vision is an essential if we are to enjoy another springtime in our beloved Assemblies of God, and we all know that sometimes surgery by a skilled specialist is needed to rectify faults in vision. In the New Testament there is a double aspect of the work of the Spirit. The churches were both 'edified' and 'multiplied'. After times of rapid multiplication, such as occurred in Jerusalem after the Day of Pentecost, and later in Antioch and Ephesus, there was an urgent need to teach and make disciples of the converts. Led by the Spirit they acted accordingly. To a certain extent this applied in the Pentecostal Movement in the British Isles in the 1920s and 1930s. It applies today overseas in fields like Latin America where the rapid growth of the Pentecostal churches is phenomenal (our critics themselves being witnesses) and in other lands where evangelists are drawing huge crowds, as in East and West Africa and S.E. Asia. There the cry is for teachers until some of us hardly know how to contain ourselves at home. The whitened harvest can easily be wasted.

But for us in the British Isles in 1960 the urgent need is no longer edification but multiplication. If we do not increase we shall slowly die. In many assemblies gifted pastors and teachers have been edifying the same little flock for years. They

need new material upon which to exercise their
God-given gifts. The hour has struck to bend all
our efforts, under God, for multiplication. We
must increase. I shall not here discuss various
methods of evangelism. For the moment, at least,
I will leave that to those more competent than I.
But I cannot resist declaring my pleasure that
our great sister-fellowship in America has adopted
as its official policy the 'mother-church' method,
by which healthy local assemblies open branch
assemblies that ultimately become self-supporting
units. I have long advocated this method, and not
without some modest personal experience of its
success. It means that new-born efforts are within
easy reach of support. Incidentally it provides an
outlet for energies of zealous and capable members
of our assemblies. I am delighted that some of our
British assemblies have made a promising start
in this direction. We must follow it up throughout
the land.

But even methods are governed by vision. We
attempt what we think should and could be done.
None of us are to blame if we are striving by every
means in our power to encourage Pentecostal
multiplication. The final issue will always remain
with the Lord of the harvest. But we are to blame
if we have lost the vision of enlargement; if we
have become content to remain little semi-private
meetings for propagating so-called 'deeper truth';
or religious clubs for selfish enjoyment of two or
three spiritual gifts; or places of undisciplined
emotionalism; or if we regard pastorates as hob-
bies for men who want to play at being ministers
of the Gospel and lack the burning and shining
without concern for the impression it makes upon
the outsider: gifts that the Holy Ghost puts within
a truly Pentecostal servant of the living God. We
must renounce all excuses for being limited in

vision, or else renounce all claim to being called
'Pentecostal'.

I cannot close my remarks on our need of bigger
vision without stating my personal conviction
that the time has come for Assemblies of God
to have some word for the unprecedented grave
social, political and moral issues facing our own
generation in 1960. Apart from desultory attempts
to discuss our attitude to divorce one searches
our agendas in vain for anything more than
denominational business. I have felt embarrassed
when religious journals have asked me for a report
of our General Conference. We seem to say nothing
about the fearful perils of atomic warfare, on
racial discrimination, on the alarming increase
in divorce and moral laxity, on gambling, on
drink in connection with road accidents, on the
use and abuse of TV and radio, on education,
or on the general spiritual atmosphere created
by material prosperity. We seem to live in a little
world of our own.

Perhaps those among us are right who insist
that our only contribution to all these burning
questions is an intensive evangelism that tells
the individual 'Ye must be born again.' It has
become axiomatic that only converted men can
make a converted world. While that is true I
submit that it is not all the truth, at least as
regards our message. I have much sympathy
with the increasing number of intelligent younger
people among us who ask for something more
than an attitude of separation which is really
isolation. People are perplexed when a movement
that claims to be dominated by the Spirit of God
has nothing to say in reply to the questions
that thoughtful men and women are asking on
every hand. Evangelism must not be equated with
escapism. I can only respectfully repeat my belief

that there is a breadth as well as a depth in the love of God shed abroad in our hearts by the Holy Ghost given to us. We may need surgery for a wider vision.

But wider vision, healthy though I believe it must be, will not of itself produce 'another springtime' in our spiritual life. Along with breadth we need depth. If it were not so trite I would say at once that our supreme need is a new touch of God on our souls, a new outpouring of the Spirit. But because such a sentiment is so trite, and because I undertook to try and indicate anything we can do to work with God in this whole matter, I will venture to be specific.

I believe that another springtime will only come to us as we restore waiting upon God. The great and precious promise that immediately springs to our minds is Isaiah 40, verse 31 – 'They that wait upon the Lord shall renew their strength', and what is such a renewal but another springtime in the soul.

It is necessary for me to emphasise that I am not speaking about waiting-meetings or, if you prefer the word, 'receiving' meetings, for those seeking the baptism in the Holy Spirit. I mean times when the members of a local assembly, or all the ministers in a District, or groups in any place who mean business with God, gather together for no other purpose than to wait upon God. That the Lord would use such occasions to baptize in the Spirit is incidental. Their supreme value and purpose is that all who attend can be renewed in the Holy Ghost. If we have lost our taste for that kind of thing then it is a symptom that some act of divine surgery has become the more urgent.

Our assemblies have become immeasurably poorer at the deeper levels because they have

mostly dropped from their schedule of regular
meetings an evening, or other suitable occasion,
set apart for free and unhurried waiting upon God,
as distinct from prayer meetings intended primar-
ily for intercession. The Pentecostal revival was
born in just such meetings all over the world, and
it will languish and die without them. Evangelism
is an accompaniment, but never a substitute. To
recommence such meetings will require surgery
in 1960 because the weekly programme in our
hundreds of closely organised assemblies, and
the calendar of events that crowd upon us all
in our many conventions and rallies, leave room
for nothing else. We all know how difficult it has
become to squeeze in one more rally. I am sure
that a limited number of special events can be
full of inspiration and profit, but we must guard
against them producing only a fictitious appearance of spiritual life that vanishes when the crowd
disperses. In recent months I have heard prayers
that God will raise up some mighty prophet, some
outstanding leader, to be the instrument for a new
revival. If that be God's way, and it may be, then I
gladly say, Amen. Yet part of the unique quality
of the Pentecostal revival, that it shares with that
tremendous awakening in the last century that
we usually call 'the '59 revival', is that it has
had no dominant personality as its figurehead –
no Luther, no Wesley, not even an Evan Roberts.
Contrary to the mistaken ideas of many people
the Pentecostal revival was not generated by the
great evangelistic and divine healing campaigns
that began to fill the largest public halls in the
British Isles in the 1920s. The evangelists and
the campaigns were the result of the revival, not
its cause. The first springtime of the Pentecostal
Movement in the British Isles, as elsewhere, was
in the little praying groups waiting upon God all

over the land. Another springtime must come in the same way because it is God's way. In these matters His principles do not change. The spiritual reward will be immeasurable. I beg of you to remember that it is fatally easy to continue as a denomination, and indeed we now possess all the machinery needed for such a continuance, and yet die as a spiritual force for revival. This is the deepest issue we must brace ourselves to face in 1960.

But, finally, I promised to enquire if there are signs that anything that can justly be called 'another springtime' has in fact begun. In attempting a reply we must guard against mere wishful thinking. But we also must not allow a holy discontent to blind us to those impressive manifestations of the grace of God among us that I referred to earlier when I sought a diagnosis of our spiritual condition. There is much blessing among us; there is a definite feeling that we are on the verge of another springtime, even it if had not yet already begun. The birds are singing; the sun is shining brightly in our sky, and our sowers are busy with the good seed of the word of God. In due season we shall reap, if we faint not.

Just here it is particularly to the point that we recognise our spiritual unity with the millions of fellow-participants in this Pentecostal revival throughout the world. If at the moment there is nothing particularly outstanding to which we can point in the British Isles, yet we must take note that prominent leaders in the historic denominations are commenting on the phenomenal growth of the Pentecostal churches in other lands. Billy Graham, speaking to a gathering of ministers, quoted Dr van Dusen's statement that, 'The Pentecostals are the fastest growing movement in Protestantism today' and went on to say that,

'We need to learn once again what it means to be baptized in the Holy Spirit.' Only just across the North Sea, one could almost say within sight of Skegness, in conservative Holland, T.L. Osborn was God's instrument in 1958 for mammoth meetings that stirred the nation. We have some of the fruit of it in gifted young Dutch students at Kenley. I can respectfully recommend you to the magazine *Pentecost* for further news about these things.

Another striking change that is taking place is in the way this Pentecostal revival is now touching those outside the official Pentecostal Movement. News of this is coming in so quickly that it is difficult to keep up with it. David du Plessis seems to have a special ministry entrusted to him by the Lord on this line. He has been asked to speak to leaders in universities and ecumenical conferences. Strangely enough some of the so-called 'liberal' theologians are more open to receive both the Pentecostal witness and the Pentecostal blessing in its fullness than those of our esteemed brethren in the fundamentalist camp. There is such a deep and widespread hunger to know the fullness of the Spirit, and such a recognition that it is the church's greatest need. You will recall the thrilling things told us on this very platform last year by Walter McAlister of Canada. We have students at Kenley, fully baptized in the Spirit, from other denominations. The atmosphere has changed where the obloquy attached to being 'Pentecostal' is concerned. A new era appears to be dawning for that revival of the manifestations of the Holy Spirit that for the last fifty years has been associated almost exclusively with the Pentecostal Movement. Can we rise by the grace of God to the challenge and the responsibility of a new situation? We must shed our complexes, bred by the ostracism of half-a-century, and boldly take our place alongside our brethren in Christ in the older denominations who may now surprise us by their openness to new movings of God's Spirit. To share in such a new springtime of Pentecostal grace and power will be thrilling.

And so I return to the opening words of my message found in Psalm 110 'Thy people shall be willing in the day of Thy power.' Another version has it – 'Your people will offer themselves freely on the day You lead Your host.' The Lord is leading His host. We will offer ourselves freely for faith and obedience. By God's grace we will share in the 'dew of His youth' in this matter of another springtime in the Pentecostal revival.

Chapter 16 – Closing Years

In 1964, shortly after leaving Kenley, Donald Gee remarried. He was seventy-three years old. His wife was Jean Coombe who herself had been widowed for many years and, interestingly, had been a member of Gee's assembly in Edinburgh during his pastorate there in the 1920s. After their marriage in Edinburgh conducted by Pastor F.R. Barnes, an old friend of Gee's, they went to live at Lindfield in Sussex.

As well as retirement from the Bible College, Gee had already retired in 1962 from a number of life-long major committee posts within the British Assemblies of God. He had been a founder-member of that denomination back in 1924 and for nearly forty years had served on the Executive Council as well as the Overseas Mission Council. Eight times he had been elected to chair the annual conference as well as being for a period editor of the official magazine *Redemption Tidings*. Almost single-handedly he had produced the first *Redemption Tidings Hymn Book*, used widely in many churches, and was chairman of the Committee producing a major revision in the 1950s.

During his retirement Gee remained as editor of *Pentecost* and continued to write regularly for several magazines. Indeed, only a week before his death, what must have been one of his final pieces of writing appeared in *Redemption Tidings*. Similarly he maintained a wide range of ministry engagements mainly in Britain, but also on the continent. He gave a week's Bible teaching in Hamburg and spoke to over a

thousand in the congregation at the Pentecostal Gypsy
Convention during a hot weekend in Dieppe.

In the midst of all this busy life Gee's death came
somewhat suddenly and peacefully. As he would have
wished it, he died in harness. On 20 July 1966 he had
attended the funeral of a life-long friend, W.S. Bradley,
in Bedford. The burial had taken place in the same
cemetery where Gee's first wife, Ruth, was buried.
Colleagues at the funeral had noticed how tired he
appeared and he had assured them that he would
take a taxi to cross London and spend the next day in
bed. He arrived in London at about 7 o'clock and took
a taxi for London Bridge Station. During the journey
he suffered a heart attack and was dead on arrival at
Guy's Hospital.

Tributes came in from all over the world wishing to
honour the memory of a truly international Pentecostal
leader. At his funeral in the Metropolitan Tabernacle
in London a large crowd filled the building. Leaders
representing a wide range of the Pentecostal movement gathered alongside colleagues from within the
Assemblies of God and other church organisations.

John Carter, a fellow Pentecostal leader, who had
known and worked with Gee for some fifty years,
preached the funeral address. His concluding words
are among the most fitting.

A gifted writer has laid down his pen. An eminent
Bible expositor will teach no more. A distinguished
editor has vacated his chair. A renowned author
has concluded his last volume. A veteran leader
has left our ranks. A great warrior has fought
his last battle. Our friend Donald has fallen
asleep. Divine awakening will bring about joyous
re-union. (*Redemption Tidings*, 12 August 1966)

After the funeral service a simple burial service took

place in Cuckfield in Sussex, near to Gee's home. And
so his work was ended.

After his death people sought to assess and categorise
his various contributions to the Pentecostal movement.
Terms such as 'great statesman', 'bridge builder'
and even Professor Walter Hollenweger's 'Pentecostal
gentleman' were some of the captions used. To many
within the Pentecostal movement he was affectionately
known as the 'apostle of balance' because of his wise and
cautious teaching in areas where fanaticism sometimes
took hold. There is no doubt that for many both within
and without the movement Gee was the sane and
acceptable face of Pentecostalism. This came out in the
funeral tribute by Gilbert Kirby, the former principal
of London Bible College, who related:

> We have a Theological Study Group presided over
> by John Stott and one of the original members
> and one of the most faithful attenders was Donald
> Gee – no one more beloved. Everyone who came
> in touch with him realised they were in touch
> with a man of God. A great bridge builder. He
> moved in wide circles. Not a contentious man,
> but a gracious, man, full of grace and truth: a
> Christian gentleman.

In summary, there is little doubt that Donald Gee
made a significant contribution within the Pentecostal
movement. His wide experience stemming from the
earliest days of the revival and his contacts with such
men as Cecil Polhill, Alexander Boddy and Smith
Wigglesworth gave him unique insight into the beginnings and development of Pentecostalism in Britain.
The period of international travel that dominated his
ministry in the 1930s again gave him a perspective
and knowledge of leaders and churches almost unsur-
passed within the movement. This all enabled him

to write what is still the best first-hand account of Pentecostalism: *Wind and Flame*.

Flowing out of this itinerant ministry came a number of valuable books revealing the influential and balanced teaching of Gee. His strategic linking of spiritual gifts with various ministries, both being enhanced by the fruit of the Spirit, is perhaps his most original and abiding contribution. Much of this teaching was then distilled in his post as principal of the Kenley Bible College, where his formative influences could be passed on to a rising generation of Pentecostal leaders.

The high-water mark of his international status came with his appointment as editor of the magazine of the World Pentecostal Conference: *Pentecost*. This, together with his place on the planning committee of that same group, turned Gee into an international statesman within the Pentecostal movement. Through his regular editorials he broadened and challenged the thinking of Pentecostal leaders in a remarkable manner. Thomas Zimmerman the General Superintendent of the American Assemblies of God spoke of Gee's writing as 'pungent and incisive'.

It must not be overlooked, however, that Gee was British and, despite his travels made a lasting contribution to the Assemblies of God in his own country. He brought stability and wisdom to the whole range of councils and committees to which he was regularly appointed. Similarly, as his conference address 'Another Springtime' has shown, he was not afraid to stir and challenge his denomination to greater vision and action.

Gee never promoted the cult of personality. His last editorial in *Pentecost*, published shortly after his death, discussed the dangers of that very issue. For him the person of the Holy Spirit and the Spirit's testimony to Christ were the significant emphases that the Pentecostal movement should be making. Indeed a renewed interest in the writings and ministry of

Donald Gee, which would be of great value to the modern Pentecostal movement with all its continuing need for balanced and mature teaching, would do just that. For Gee's ministry pointed consistently and biblically to the Holy Spirit and through him to Christ.

Books by Donald Gee

Concerning Spiritual Gifts (Springfield, Mo. 1928)
The Ministry-Gifts of Christ (Springfield, Mo. 1930)
Concerning Shepherds and Sheepfolds (London 1930)
The Fruit of the Spirit (Springfield, Mo. 1934)
God's Grace and Power for Today (Springfield Mo. 1935)
Studies in Guidance (London 1936)
Laughter and Tears
Proverbs for Pentecost
This is the Will of God – the Bible and Sexual Problems (London 1940)
Bonnington Toll – And After (London 1943)
Why Pentecost? (London 1944)
Keeping in Touch (London 1951)
Trophimus I Left Sick (London 1952)
Spiritual Gifts in the Work of the Ministry Today (Springfield, Mo. 1965)
Fruitful or Barren? (Springfield, Mo. 1961)
Toward Pentecostal Unity (Springfield Mo. 1961)
Wind and Flame (London 1967)
These Men I Knew (Nottingham 1980)